EXPAT EDUCATION

An Expat's Guide to
Choosing a School Overseas

Carole Hallett Mobbs

For Rhiannon

CONTENTS

ABOUT THE AUTHOR

Carole Hallett Mobbs is the mother of a teenager, a 'trailing spouse', ex-expat, writer and Expat Life Mentor.

She lived overseas for twelve years and has recently repatriated to the UK. Carole supported her daughter through all the moves and several changes of school and is well-equipped to guide you through the intricacies of choosing a school abroad for your child.

Carole is the founder of ExpatChild.com, the go-to website for many thousands of families moving abroad with children. ExpatChild was launched in 2012 to provide useful and practical advice about relocation preparation and expat parenting topics. She now runs three expat websites;

- expatchild.com
- expatchild.com/expatdirectory
- expatability.net

Her passion for helping parents move abroad by sharing practical and logical advice, along with not sugar-coating the realities of expat life, led her to create The Expatability Club, which allows her to provide personalised and targeted guidance to truly help people making the move overseas. Using a common-sense approach and her natural problem-solving skills, Carole will help you navigate the challenges of moving and living overseas.

WHAT IS EXPATABILITY?

EXPAT

A person who lives outside their native country.

ABILITY

Possession of the means or skill to do something. Talent, skill, or proficiency in a particular area.

HOW CAN I HELP YOU WITH *YOUR* MOVE OVERSEAS?

I will help you navigate the challenges of moving and living overseas with no-nonsense, practical and sensible advice. I'll help you aim for complete Expat Ability!

While I can't make your decisions for you, I can offer experience-based suggestions, recommendations, tools and tips to lighten your mental and emotional load. Consider me a combination of Virtual Assistant, Expat Life Mentor and your best friend!

Visit Expatability.net for more information, or email me at hello@expatability.net

I look forward to chatting with you soon,

Carole

WHY 'AN EXPAT'S GUIDE TO CHOOSING A SCHOOL OVERSEAS'?

When we first moved overseas, we didn't think much about education for our daughter. Actually, that's not true, of course, because education is such an important and pivotal part of anyone's life, but we had very little choice in most aspects of our new life abroad.

Due to the nature of my husband's job and employer, we must live where we are told, in accommodation we don't even see until we arrive in that country and we were informed that she should go to a specific school. As the company were paying the fees, we had to go with that. Since then, the company's policies have relaxed a little and we ended our expat life with more opportunities to self-select a school that suited her better. Hopefully you will have much more choice at the outset of your expat adventure!

I remember arriving in Tokyo on a grey Wednesday afternoon, November 2006. Exhausted, excited, trepidatious, and trying to parent an extremely lively five-year-old who didn't quite understand our impending adventure.

We had done our best to prepare her for the big move, but she clearly hadn't comprehended the vast distance between the UK and Japan, because she kept asking questions like, *"Can my friends come over for a sleepover tomorrow?"*.

What had we done? Were we making the right move? (Answer – yes, of course, but all kinds of thoughts hit your mind in that situation!).

This wasn't my first trip abroad by any means. I'd travelled all over the world, for business and pleasure – often solo, for many years long before our daughter was born, often for months at a time. My husband spent most of his adult life almost continually travelling on business too.

Neither was this like an ordinary family vacation; a temporary stay we could simply leave early if things weren't to our liking. But neither of us had ever *lived* overseas before. And living abroad is a very different experience in so many ways.

Our move to Tokyo was a planned, four year posting as part of my husband's career. We were completely relocating to a new and, in this case, an extremely 'foreign' home, starting our daughter in a new school, learning a new language, a new culture, acquiring a taste for new food – a new everything. It was both exciting and daunting. For me, it would be even more as an entirely new life as a trailing spouse. Or more accurately, the *accompanying* spouse – I do not 'trail'! I'd had to give up my business in the UK in order to move overseas.

Looking back, I can say that with the invaluable help of new expat friends, neighbours and a very large dose of trial and error, we not only survived the next few years, we absolutely thrived. Japan will always be in all our hearts. In the end, we stayed for nearly five years, leaving a month after the Great Tohoku earthquake of March 2011.

Our next posting took us to Berlin for two years and then on to South Africa for four and a half years before repatriating back to the UK in February 2018. Twelve years overseas! Repatriating was interesting…

Each move has had its triumphs and troubles and there have been as many similarities as there have been things we would do differently, if only we had known.

One overriding concern remained a constant throughout; our desire to make the transition from former 'home' to new 'home' as seamless as possible. To help our daughter adapt to each host school and to make each experience an enriching, rewarding one.

Moving to a new house is a huge step for anyone. In fact, it's reportedly the third most stressful event after death and divorce! I can personally confirm this is true.

When you move to a new country, yes, it's an exciting adventure, but with the best intentions in the world, the whole experience is challenging in many ways. Move overseas with your children and it takes your stress levels to an entirely new level altogether. Hence the idea for this guide.

Sometimes, not having a choice is easier than having too much. While we had no choice in which school our daughter attended in Tokyo, having *no* choice wasn't plain sailing. When issues occurred, we were unable to make changes, due to the restrictions placed on us from the employers. In later moves we had a few more school options available, but that's not particularly helpful when the few schools we *could* choose from were *all* unsuitable.

A crystal ball would have been extremely useful! Of course, hindsight is always clear. Having said that, the issues we experienced could have occurred at any school in the world, so this isn't a comment on specific countries. We've learned many lessons from our encounters with various schools abroad, and I've endeavoured to pack as much advice into this guide as is feasibly possible.

I wish I had this book when I first became an expat parent.

My hope is that when you navigate the many decisions you will face regarding your child's education abroad this guide will help you do so as effectively and efficiently as possible.

With very best wishes to you, for a stress-free relocation overseas. Or, to be honest, an *almost* stress-free relocation!

Don't forget, if you're considering or planning a move overseas and you'd like some personalised advice about choosing a school abroad, or any other aspect of your relocation, please do get in touch with me at hello@expatability.net

A DIFFICULT DECISION MADE EASIER FOR YOU

Choosing the right school for your child is one of the hardest decisions you'll make as a parent when relocating overseas.

- Do you go for an international school or a local school?
- Which international school system?
- Will the language barrier be too much if you choose a local school?
- Perhaps home-schooling would be better all round? But did you know that home education is illegal in some countries?
- What about your child's future? Will you be moving back home at some point, or will you be moving to another country? Do you even know yet?!

Perhaps it would be best just to send them to the school that all the other expats go to? After all, it's all about the experience of living abroad, isn't it? All schools are the basically the same anyway... Yes, I have actually heard this said. Scary, isn't it?

Children are individuals with different needs and personalities. There certainly isn't one-size-fits-all education option for expat children.

There are many education options around for expats, and so much depends on your individual family set-up and child that there is no 'one-school-fits-all' solution. Each child is different and each country's school system is different, even within the 'generic' international schools. Also, families differ in their requirements and aspirations, and even relocations vary greatly. What worked well for you all in one country won't necessarily be replicated in your next move.

It's easy to get very stressed at this point. Don't panic! I've put together this book to help you kick-start your search for the best type of school for *your* child.

There are many considerations and details you need to brainstorm, so I've detailed them in this book for you. I also include a list of questions you may find useful to ask when you have narrowed down your school choice. You'll get a great insight into just what is involved in making the right choice for your family,

Choosing a school for your expat child can be a trial and it all boils down to a very personal decision. A decision that, as parents, we can only hope is for the best.

HOW DOES EXPAT LIFE AFFECT YOUR CHILD'S EDUCATION?

Education is not just about going to school and getting a degree. It's about widening your knowledge and absorbing the truth about life.
Shakuntala Devi

One of the biggest worries for any parent choosing to move their family overseas is how will this decision affect their children's ability to achieve academically. All over the world, a good education is viewed as paramount to success, but how can we ensure our children get this when the country we are moving to may not uphold the same values as our native nation would?

And besides that, if you move around a bit, will moving them between schools damage them forever? You can't help but think that, but in my experience, this concern seems to be emphasised exclusively by people at home who have never moved and will probably never move, ever.

In many ways, a foreign education is a huge benefit to our children, as they will gain breadth and different knowledge which their peers at home will be missing out on.

But what about the things they do not gain? Should we be worried that this education is different from that which we know back home, and how will we ensure they can slot back into society if and when they return to their native country?

THE IMPACT OF EXPAT LIFE ON LEARNING

Your child may learn about the Romans three times, but never know how to work out percentages.

If you move regularly from country to country, you need to make sure that some sort of continuity of education can happen. Otherwise, your child may learn about the Romans three times in three different schools, but never know how to work out percentages, because they always miss that lesson somehow. Unfortunately, none of us can see into the future and plans often go awry. All you can do is your best for your child.

For example, after our four years in Tokyo we fully expected to move back to the UK. However, my husband then got a transfer to Berlin. The transfer date changed, and changed, and changed. At various points during our final year in Tokyo I had to find a permanent school in our home county in England; then a temporary school in the same area; then a very short-term school in my Mother's home county and even considered a spell of home education. As it happened, we stayed in Tokyo for a further six months and moved directly to Germany with no 'stop-over' in the UK at all. Needless to say, I now have a huge experience of choosing schools!

If you *know* you will return to your home country while your child is still of school age, try to work out what stage of their education they are likely to be at, because school admissions can often be impossible during critical exam years. This is particularly relevant in secondary education in England, Wales and Northern Ireland with regards to GCSE exams. Especially with all the governmental changes these exams are seeing in recent years.

The answers to these sorts of questions are neither clear, nor easy, but with a little foresight we can at least weigh up the pros and cons of taking our children abroad, so that we go into our move with informed and open eyes.

THE DISADVANTAGES OF EXPAT EDUCATION FOR CHILDREN

Social and Cultural Differences

Making new friends is always tough but trying to make new friends among people who have been brought-up entirely differently, have different interests and potentially speak a different language, is exponentially harder for our children to cope with. Over time, these things can become easier, as they get used to your child, and your child gets used to them. But in the short term, don't expect much learning to be happening, as much of your child's energy will be focused on social acceptance.

Ultimately, this disadvantage will become a massive benefit to your child as they absorb different social and cultural norms and develop a natural global outlook.

A Change in Curriculum

Moving to a new school in a new country can be tough for many reasons. The main one being the curriculum. Switching between, for example, the British curriculum and the American curriculum (*and vice versa*) is easy when your children are very young, but much more difficult as they get older. It may be difficult for some children, regardless of their age, while others of the same age may struggle.

Students in the new school may have covered material your child has not, which puts your child on the back foot when it comes to mutual knowledge. Moving to another country can exacerbate this problem, meaning they are exposed to completely alien curricula and topics which never featured in their school back home. It doesn't necessarily mean it's bad or unworkable, just that the settling in period will be more difficult and potentially somewhat longer. Sometimes the teachers will take this into consideration and help the student, sometimes they will not. It's unfortunately, the luck of the draw with that particular aspect.

Depending on the number of years your child has already attended school, this may be more or less of a problem.

THE BENEFITS OF EXPAT LIFE FOR CHILDREN

New Challenges, New Skills

Expat children typically face an array of new skills and knowledge to be acquired before they can truly fit in with their new social group. Challenging it may be, but these trials will equip them with the skills and knowledge that will set them apart from other job applicants later in life.

Their breadth of experience and knowledge acquisition will become a highlight of their lives as they mature into well rounded adults.

Language and Culture

Children soak up new language and
sponge. They are so much better at a
and language of the places they visit. Yo
you're asking them what something mean
certain food, or why someone is behaving in a p
Sure, it's not the three 'R's we've become accustc
home, but surely this is learning at its most natu
greatest, in the way it should always be done?

Changing school is always a stressful time for a child of any
age, and when that school change comes with a complete
change of lifestyle, peer group, language and other life
elements, we should expect the settling in period to be long
and probably hard.

As mentioned in a previous point, your child will learn how
to interact with many different people, and they will learn
how to do this naturally and quickly.

Don't panic that you've done the wrong thing by your
child… they *will* settle in and will love you for this challenge,
albeit probably some years into the future.

A CASE FOR RAISING CHILDREN OVERSEAS

Travel is fatal to prejudice, bigotry, and narrow-mindedness, and many of our people need it sorely on these accounts. Broad, wholesome, charitable views of men and things cannot be acquired by vegetating in one little corner of the earth all one's lifetime.
Mark Twain

Our daughter has been travelling with us since the age of five. For her, it's such a part of life that she has so far, lived in four countries and attended eight different schools.

It's not ideal, but for us, it's our life and the benefits outweigh any negatives. We're expats and our postings have so far taken us from the UK, to Japan, to Germany and to South Africa and back to the UK, twelve years on.

I'd be lying if I said it has all been a bed of roses. Uprooting the family and moving them half-way across the world is not without its challenges, some of which I detail throughout this guide. But overall, the experience for us has been an extremely positive one.

When you move abroad, there's the inevitable excitement of the move itself. It is after all an amazing adventure. It's a bit like expecting your first child. Bear with me…! When we first discover the news, we go into overdrive to research and learn everything there is to know about pregnancy. We go through that journey in a state of excitement and panic. We plan, we prepare, we buy all the 'stuff', and we pack the bag ready for the hospital. Everything leads up to the big moment – the birth. But that big moment is only just the beginning. The real life starts when you start your new life as parents.

It's the same with an overseas move: we do all the research and planning, but when it sinks in that the move is an actual relocation, you start to worry. This is not a long holiday, this is your life now.

As a parent, you naturally worry whether your child will fit in with the locals, or whether they will like your new lifestyle. You worry they'll resent you for taking them away from their friends and you worry they'll miss familiar surroundings.

In my experience, and that of other expat parents, it *does* take time to settle. But they won't resent you and they will adapt – with your help, of course.

Your children will acquire an impressive array of skills they might not have otherwise acquired. In our daughter's case, she's learnt new languages on the fly, found her way around new school systems, and caught up with different curriculums, and all this while simultaneously making new friends and negotiating life in all its forms.

She started learning Japanese at the age of five and although we are sadly no longer there, she can still recall much of it, so now has an impressive haul of languages – Japanese, German, French, Spanish, Russian and Afrikaans. Most of these have been naturally absorbed by learning from her friends.

Self-reliance is another aspect of expat life that is applicable to all age groups, even adults. It depends on the country you live in. For example, in Japan, children are extremely independent from a young age. We saw children travelling to school on their own from about six years old. Our daughter noted this and wanted to follow suit. Whilst she didn't travel to school alone, she was able to become independent from a similar age. As it's such a safe country, with complete social trust, she ran errands to the shops and post office regularly, crossing a six-lane road by herself and chattering happily to people she met en route. In Germany, that independence was slightly curtailed due to our remote location, but she was still traveling to and from school on the public bus on her own from ten years old. Unfortunately, South Africa was too dangerous and, with no safe public transport, that well-earned and necessary independence became non-existent, simply due to safety and security there.

When we returned to the UK, she had to learn a lot of day-to-day actions the local teenagers have been doing by themselves for a few years. Thankfully, her self-sufficiency was instilled early enough in her life that this hasn't proved too difficult for her.

As challenging as some of these situations have been, she's developed an incredible resilience, is flexible and adept to change.

One skill that becomes evident very quickly is how easily expat children make friends. Put my daughter in any unusual and unknown situation and she will have found like-minded friends within minutes!

Our expat child – and so many like her – has been given a real live experience of the wider world we live in. She's had a hands-on opportunity to integrate with people of other cultures, backgrounds and beliefs and is already showing a tolerance and respect for other national groups that makes us immensely proud.

THIRD CULTURE KIDS

I often came across the expression Third Culture Kid (TCK) but admit I didn't truly understand it until I stumbled across an article in the Daily Telegraph by Ruth Van Reken[1], a second generation ATCK and international speaker on issues related to global family living, who gave some interesting insight into the phenomenon.

(Another term used in this context, is Adult Third Culture Kid (ATCK) to describe adults who had this experience as children and more recently, 'Triangles'[2], expats who experience the challenges of repatriation).

Drs. Ruth and John Useem, both sociologists and anthropologists coined the phrase Third Culture in the 1950's when they were in India, initially to study the roles of Indians studying abroad.

While there, they observed Americans living and working as Foreign Service officers, missionaries, businessmen, media representatives and similar roles. They also observed the behaviour of children attending schools set up for them, to accompany their parents abroad.

Dr. Useem discovered that these families formed a cross-cultural lifestyle of shared experiences, what she called a 'third culture', one that was entirely different to either the first culture of their homeland, or the second culture of their host country.

Dr. Useem is widely regarded as the founder of TCK and ATCK research, and has published many doctoral dissertations and papers, which make fascinating reading.[3]

Of course, things have changed considerably since then, a time when expat families settled together in one area, or when companies had no option but to form make-shift camp schools, exclusively for the children of their employees who worked there.

Today, international careers take us from one country to another. Our children who follow suit benefit from a far greater choice in the school options available to them, allowing them to truly experience international life to the full.

It's quite likely the experience of traveling and living abroad will shape them emotionally and psychologically for the better, not to mention the positive way in which they will view the world, something that will be of tremendous benefit to us in their becoming our future international politicians, ambassadors, entrepreneurs and such like.

Consider perhaps the world's most famous TCK, President Barack Obama[4], the 44th president of the United States of America and the first African-American to have served as president. He was born and raised in Hawaii to a mother from Kansas and father from Kenya, he also spent four years in Indonesia (as his step-father was Indonesian).

In common with other expats, Obama had and indeed still has, a big-picture world view that media pundits (who tried to pigeon-hole him into a single identifying cultural trait) at first failed to understand. As Ruth Van Reken noted in this article for the Daily Beast[5] online,

"Obama's former colleagues on the Harvard Law Review were among the first to note both his exceptional skill at mediating among competing arguments and the aloofness that made his own views hard to discern. That cool manner of seeming "above it all" is also a classic feature of the Third Culture Kid."

The article went on to explain how TCKs' ability to meet various challenges (in culture, identity, and so forth) contribute to their ability to take the positive from those experiences and create a keen sense of *"This is who I am, no matter where I am."*

Another notable TCK is British Actor, Colin Firth[6] *('Pride and Prejudice', 'The Kingsman', 'Bridget Jones Diary')*. Firth was born in Grayshott, Hampshire, UK, to parents who were both academics and teachers. In fact, he's a second generation TCK – both his parents were raised in India, because his maternal and paternal grandparents were missionaries overseas.

Firth travelled a lot due to his parents' work. His father was a history lecturer and education officer for the Nigerian Government, so Firth spent many years in Nigeria. He also lived in St. Louis, Missouri, which he described as "a difficult time", before returning to England. He was still an outsider and the target of bullying. To counter this, he feigned a local working-class accent and copied his schoolmates' lack of interest in schoolwork. Perhaps this led to a taste of acting, as he joined a drama workshop and acting school shortly after. The rest as they say, is history.

Okay, so it's nice to have a little glitzy gossip, but that doesn't mean being a TCK is without its challenges.

While TCKs will have a world view of belonging everywhere, they will also feel they belong nowhere. They'll find the classic question, *"Where are you from?"* confusing, because despite the country of their birth, they're not from one place in the way others who haven't travelled are. A TCK's back-story will likely involve a complicated tapestry of places.

THE CHALLENGE OF REPATRIATION

Repatriation is another challenge. All expats who return to their home country are supposed to feel instantly 'settled' once they repatriate. After all, as far as friends and family are concerned, you have returned 'home'. Yet 'settled' is often the last thing anyone feels upon repatriation, with an expat child or TCK feeling it harder than adults. They've left a home they were used to, travelled somewhere new, partly adopted its customs and cultures and then repatriated to what, exactly? Somewhere they're not entirely familiar with, among people they no longer entirely understand (or who no longer understand them) and yet they – and you – are expected to slot in with no problems at all.

A huge detail to recognise on behalf of our children is this: while living overseas may have been a mere fraction of our adult life, it probably makes up most, if not all, of our child's life experience. With that in mind, it is important to realise that they will view repatriation in an entirely different way from us. As far as your child is concerned, repatriation may as well be the same as 'simply' another relocation to a different country.

And here's an interesting quirk. In our case, although our family is British, my daughter has lived overseas for over two thirds of her life. Her personal culture is completely global. And her language is a delightful and unique mixture of Americanisms, Japanese words, Afrikaans sayings and unusual sentence structures. This is partly due to her speaking different languages throughout her life and partly due to having multicultural friends whose first language is *not* English. This was especially noticeable when she was younger in Japan and Germany, as the sentence structure of both languages are surprisingly similar. And even now she uses phrases unique to South Africa, such as "I'll tell you *just now*", meaning "I'll tell you in a minute". We have quite a few impromptu British English lessons at home!

There are some aspects of 'Britishness' that completely elude her, such as British expressions, "When pigs fly", or "Once in a blue moon," to name just a couple. She doesn't watch British TV, particularly the very popular reality shows. Neither does she follow the celebrity culture that seems to pervade her age-group, which makes it tricky for her to find mutual discussion topics with her peers. Teens here in the UK seem to prefer to pigeonhole their mates, often starting with the question "What music are you into?". She doesn't know how to answer that using English genres right now. Certainly not the life-shattering experience some people lead us to believe we inflict on our children when we move overseas.

Thankfully, she is comfortable with her uniqueness and understands why and how her upbringing is different from those who have lived in one place all their lives.

Another cultural difference example: Christmas can be confusing for little ones. In Japan, it wasn't a recognised holiday at all and is a normal working day, while in Germany it's celebrated with all the trappings. She once asked, "Who is right?" and of course, there is no correct answer to that at all. It's occurrences like this that you simply don't expect when you move overseas. It opens your eyes to a refreshing, different and unique outlook into other cultures and life in general.

But in many ways, in common with other TCKs, she has her own personal culture. There's no concept of being different due to nationality, race or creed. Instead, she feels a connection to *people*, which in my opinion is a fantastic way to be.

A DIVERSE AND UNIQUE EDUCATION

In the second of many of Dr. Useem's studies on expats and TCKs, she found that students who lived overseas during childhood, were four times more likely to attain a university degree than those who hadn't.[7] The study in 1991, of 700 people (ranging from 25 to 84 years of age), returned some interesting results.

Only 21 percent of the American population (24 percent of men and 18 percent of women) had graduated from a four-year college. In contrast, 81 percent of adult TCKs earned at least a bachelor's degree (87 percent of the men, 76 percent of the women), and half of that number went on to earn master's degrees or doctorates.

A clue as to why expats and TCKs are more likely to earn higher degrees, can perhaps be found in the way they do it. In many cases, there were characteristics of continuing their education while 'opportunities came up', such as "translating full-time for a professor outside their major", or "burning around Africa – a place I haven't seen." They were even keen to continue their higher education later in life, after taking time out to get married and have children.

Why do I mention this? Because rather than worry your child might be missing out due of your seemingly nomadic lifestyle, studies like this show that expats and TCKs are highly intelligent, innovative and creative people, driven by the cross-cultural opportunities they experience in their travels. Your child will have a broader world view than their peers who stayed in one country or even town for their entire lives, one that will contribute to them becoming true global citizens.

It's something my own expat family has experienced thus far. We have a treasure trove of wild, wacky and wonderful memories. And because we've been through everything together, we've become very close to each other.

When you spend most of your life travelling overseas, often with no extended family nearby to give a helping hand, you're naturally drawn closer together to encourage each other, cry together and even have a good old laugh together.

And trust me, there's plenty to laugh about when you're learning a new language or trying to learn how to exist in a new culture. Try buying medicine from the pharmacy, for example. You cannot be shy. Have you ever tried asking for medication for a stomach upset when you can't think of the right words in the local vocabulary? You become excellent at miming – and necessarily shameless! The ability to laugh at yourself is a big benefit in expat life.

Raising a child overseas is an amazing opportunity – for you and for them – and this guide is designed to help you enhance that opportunity, by finding a school environment that is just right for them.

A POTENTIAL NEGATIVE TO MOVING ABROAD WITH CHILDREN

Aim for success, not perfection. Never give up your right to be wrong, because then you will lose the ability to learn new things and move forward with your life. Remember that fear always lurks behind perfectionism.
David M. Burns

I've mentioned in brief, the positive side of moving and travelling abroad, it would be remiss of me to *not* mention any downsides.

EXPAT CHILD SYNDROME

One of those downsides, at least for your child, is something psychologists and therapists refer to as Expat Child Syndrome (ECS). It is a term that is used to describe the emotional stress *some* children experience when they move abroad.

Moving abroad is a big step in anyone's life. It's an exciting new chapter and of course, a new adventure. Yet it can stir up feelings of apprehension. It will mean a new home – will you like it? A new neighbourhood – will you fit in, will anyone like you? A new language – will you learn to speak it and how will you cope if no-one understands you?

It's a smörgåsbord of new challenges and you won't know how they'll pan out until you get there. There are always challenges and hurdles when moving to a new location, and your children will face challenges too, albeit of a different kind.

Imagine how your child will feel about the move, if they don't fully comprehend why you're moving? It's all very well you telling them, *"We have to move because of mum/dad's career,"* but do they understand, really?

Expat Grief

Being separated from the familiar – relatives, friends, surroundings, home – is something most children won't have experienced before. Those feelings of separation can be so acute, they have been likened to the loss experienced due to grief.

It's not an exaggeration to say that it can almost be a period of mourning for a child (and adult, for that matter) when they move to a new place and leave everything they know behind.

The Expat Grieving Process

The leaving of friendships and familiarity is a recognised form of grief, also known as 'expat grief' or 'relocation grief'. Children often grieve in silence or try to ignore the loss associated with change because they don't have the necessary understanding of their own feelings.

Generally, the accepted stages of grief are denial, anger, bargaining, depression and acceptance. Similar stages can sometimes be seen in expat children, so keep your eye on them to help them through this time.

Ensuring your child says a healthy goodbye helps your family to look forward and achieve real closure. Goodbyes are important and are vital for healthy progression.

Encourage your child to communicate, and make sure you listen out for the unspoken. Be honest – don't make promises you can't keep. Let them know that your family unit will remain strong and supportive despite the changes taking place. Focus on the positive aspects but don't be afraid to address the negative too. Above all, be supportive, and reassure your child that they can cope with what's ahead, no matter how old they are.

Ruth E. Van Reken[8], explains the loss in this way:

"Many of their losses are not visible or recognised by others. With no language or understanding to process these losses, many TCKs never learned how to deal with them as they happened and the grief comes out in other ways e.g. denial, anger, depression, extreme busyness, etc."

WHAT ISSUES DO EXPAT CHILDREN FACE?

New and unfamiliar situations can be intimidating, and sometimes even traumatic, for people of all ages, and this is even more so the case for children who don't fully understand the move to a new location nor do they know what to expect. This feeling of unsettledness can be a huge challenge for a lot of children.

Of course, making new friends is one of the biggest hurdles, especially for children who are shy or have language barriers to contend with. It can take one little thing, such as a difficult day at a new school, to make a child go into their shell and miss their home country and their old friends deeply.

You also need to recognise that you are likely to be much busier than usual, as you will be dealing with your own adjustment process, having taken on a new home and job for example, which can make the child feel even more alone.

The more you understand ECS, the better equipped you'll be to help your child cope if they suffer from it.

While there isn't a list of symptoms, here are typical ways in which ECS can manifest itself:

Behavioural Changes

A child may become unusually withdrawn, showing signs of loneliness and seclusion, or they may be disruptive or un-cooperative. This could be down to feelings of anger or resentment ('you've removed them from familiar surroundings'), or feelings of loss ('they're missing their familiar surroundings').

Social Challenges

ECS seems to be most common in children at puberty age. They're already going through physical and emotional changes and they're often reliant on their close friends of the same age. Removing them from their social circle at this age can have a significant impact. With support, ECS usually disappears over time, but if not, it can result in a child struggling to fit in with social circles at all.

Possible Causes of ECS

I should stress that it is impossible to predict ECS. While it is something your child *could* experience, that does not mean they *will*.

However, where children have been identified as suffering from ECS, this is what they have in common:

Age

As mentioned previously, the age of your child has the biggest impact. Moving abroad with babies and young children is markedly easier than moving with older children. Puberty, and its associated changes, can make settling in more difficult for them. Moving with teenagers can be even more problematic unless they are used to moving around regularly.

Frequent Relocation

Continually relocating or moving on every couple of years (e.g. where families are diplomats or in the armed forces, for example), can clearly have an impact on a child's emotions. After all, they begin to settle into a new location and are then expected to move on again shortly afterwards. It can be frustrating and upsetting for them, if they feel they've worked hard at trying to fit in.

Location

Another factor seems to be location, whether the country they're moving to appears to be drastically different to their home or former host country. Entirely unfamiliar customs or cultures e.g. from East to West, or vice versa, developed country to developing country, can have an impact on their bearing. Not surprisingly, if they're moving to what may seem like the other side of the world, they may feel as if they'll never see their friends or family again.

School

Choosing a suitable school is clearly a key factor and the need for this guide. Moving schools is daunting for any child in any circumstance, let alone for someone who's moving to an entirely new country. Suffice to say, it's something that requires careful research, while you weigh up your family's circumstances and of course, the needs of your child.

HOW TO SUPPORT A CHILD WITH ECS

One thing you will have noticed about the above factors where ECS can occur, is they're difficult to change, especially in the context of living the expat life. If you need to travel, you need to travel. There's clearly nothing you can do about that.

It's vital to stress that ECS is impossible to predict and prevent, as it's something all expat children *can* experience, but not all expat children *will*. And of course, children can experience mental health problems regardless of their upbringing and location in the world.

You will never know what may have transpired if you *hadn't* moved overseas and it's conceivable that your child may have experienced difficulties anyway. It's crucially important that you understand this and not beat yourself up about it.

What you can do however, is be prepared and aware so you can help your child cope with the challenges that arise from moving abroad.

Communicate

Communication is one of the key components to ensuring a smooth transition. You need to watch your children's behaviour to pick up on any symptoms of ECS. Talk with your children frequently and actually *listen* to what they are saying and acknowledge any frustrations they may be experiencing. Often you need to listen to what your child *doesn't* say. Read between the lines.

Don't dismiss your child as 'acting up', as if they seemingly didn't want to move abroad in the first place.

Take time out to talk to them about what they're feeling and more importantly, to listen to what they're telling you. It's easy to become wrapped up in your own adjustment process as a parent. Your child needs an outlet for their feelings too. Often simple acknowledgement of your child's feelings and the struggles they are encountering can be a massive step in helping them to deal with the emotional stress they are experiencing.

Help Them Create a New Network

They'll be leaving a network of close friends behind. The first step in helping them adjust, is for you to become actively involved in the local neighbourhood yourself, as opposed to hiding away from the locals and only socialising with other expats.

You don't have to force it. Gently encourage them to get involved by, for example, inviting your local neighbours in for a coffee. If you have children of a similar age, all the better. It's the best way to learn more about the neighbourhood (aka the local gossip) or what schools are like from a local's point of view.

It's equally as important to keep in contact with old friends back home, so that your child doesn't feel entirely cut off. A key factor to being able to develop new relationships, is for them to feel they're likeable – by old friends and new.

Adjust to New Traditions While Retaining Old

Similarly, keep up with 'old' traditions while you embrace the new. That might mean cooking the foods you're accustomed to (if available), while acquiring a taste for the new cuisine. Or celebrating your usual holidays, while learning the customs of your host country. As insignificant as these might seem, they're one step closer to your child bridging the gap between what they've left behind and what they're getting used to.

In summary, don't panic and don't assume that by relocating abroad, you will cause emotional stress in your child.

If you do encounter any problems, it's important that you act immediately. Seek professional help and choose your professional wisely. Try to find someone who has experience of TCK issues or is at least willing to learn and be open to the differences.

Now that you're aware of ECS, simply store it away in your toolbox to use if the need arises.

HOW DO YOU DECIDE ON A
SCHOOL IN ANOTHER COUNTRY?

Learning is a treasure that will follow its owner everywhere.
Chinese Proverb

Regardless of where you live, whether you're moving abroad or not, choosing a school for your child can be difficult. You have no idea how your child will take to education and you have no idea how good a school really is until your child is there and experiencing it for themselves.

Of course, you may not have any choices and there may be only one school in your area so that's where your child will go. It was like this where I grew up in the rural depths of England – there was one school and that was it. But if you're moving to a different country you do usually have a choice of education type. By 'type' I mean, what kind of education system will you choose? Local schools? International schools? Home education?

Let's examine this further and look at how to drill down to discover what type of education will work for you and your child.

So much depends on individuality that it's hard to write a definitive guide to making that choice. But I've given it my best shot. This chapter will go through the basics of choice and considerations, while subsequent sections will take a deeper look at your options, with some real-life examples from other expat parents.

YOUR CHILD

First and foremost, we are talking about *your* child. Not mine, not your colleague's, not your friend's, not someone on an internet forum, *your* child. It's important to remember that each child is different, each country's school system is different, and each family differs in their requirements and wishes. If you have two children, they will have very different personalities. Each child's character is entirely different from all others. You are choosing a school for *your* child, *your* family.

This cannot be emphasised enough, and yet, you'll be reading this, shaking your head and saying, "Well, that's ridiculously obvious. I know this! Why are you telling me something I already know?".

Bear with me… Countless times I hear people quoting clichés such as, "Children are resilient", "Children adapt".

Many people believe a cliché is a fact. However, the definition of cliché is, 'a phrase or opinion that is overused and betrays a lack of original thought'.

Not all children are resilient. Not all children adapt.

Many do adapt, but it is dangerous to assume all will and to ignore their uniqueness.

Making this assumption – that your child is resilient and will adapt to whatever life throws at them – can set up your child, and by extension, your family, for numerous problems. Choosing a school for your child based on where your colleague's child went five years ago, or because it's the school all the other expats use, is potentially setting up your child for difficulties. I'm not saying this *will* happen, but it might. You know your child best, so use your own judgement when choosing a school for them.

What is your child's personality? Their character? Are they robust or sensitive? Extrovert or introvert? Are they sporty and energetic? Or academic and quiet? Or sporty and quiet – academic and energetic? Do they have specific hobbies or play a certain musical instrument? Is the school able to enable them to continue these? What aspects of their personality need nurturing? What are their vulnerabilities and what are their strengths?

Carefully consider your own child's need when it comes to choosing a school. Someone else's child may be doing well at that school because their personality fits the school's ethos. This may not be the case for your child.

Moving between countries will highlight cultural differences in education and expectations and there are too many variables involved that it's impossible for me to say, "You must choose this school." Nevertheless, you will find there are a few people who *will* say this to you! I've not worked out why this happens, but it does. And they get offended if you don't take their advice. Just do your own thing.

That being said, there are some more practical questions that you need to consider before deciding on the *type* of education you all need. And you need to consider these before you choose a specific school.

How Long Are You Going to Stay in This Country?

It's really important to think ahead. Yes, I know it is impossible to know how life will pan out, I've been there! But it's vital to know your future plans as much as possible.

Do you intend to stay permanently in your new location? If this is the final stop in your expat journey a local school may be the best option for you and your child, especially if they need to learn the local language. Fully immersing them in local culture, including through their schooling, is one of the best ways to help make the transition as easy as possible for them. If you are moving for a short time – a couple of years or so – then your educational needs may well be different and governed by this knowledge.

Of course, plans change. And nobody can see into the future. You may plan to stay in one country for the entirety of your child's education, but life has a habit of getting in the way of plans. The best you can do is to make the right decision for now, with an eye on the future.

Where Are You Moving Next?

If you'll be moving elsewhere in the future, it's worth considering a school that will provide a continuity of education. An international school is an option to consider in this scenario. Alternatively, if you'll be moving back to your home country, it makes sense to choose a school overseas that runs a similar curriculum that ties in with your home country's system.

What Do You Want for Your Children in the Future?

We all dream that our tiny baby will be an academic genius with super sporting skills who will thrive in all aspects of life. We dream of them entering the best university and flying high and happy throughout life. Although I have met a proportionally high number of expat children who *do* fulfil this dream, not everyone has that child. It's best to be realistic and recognise your child's own individuality, strengths and weaknesses. Not all children go on to university, and it's important to recognise that when faced with other people's expectations. A happy child is the best outcome.

As for considering the future and possible higher education, this will depend on how old your children are when you choose a school overseas. If they are old enough to know and to have thought about it, what do they want for themselves? Do they consider specific careers and university options? Of course, if they are younger then the decision will still fall to you to give them the best possible start. And, let's be frank, that's all it is – a start.

Can You Support Your Child in a New School?

As well as supporting your children academically, it's important that you can support them throughout the transition into their new school life. There may be language barriers as well as cultural differences, particularly if they will be attending local schools. Can you speak the language well enough to discuss important matters with their teachers?

They'll also face the challenge of making new friends. You'll need to consider whether you can give them the right support with the time to support their social integration.

How Different Is the Curriculum Going to Be?

When there's a whole new curriculum to take into consideration it's important that your children are given support at home to maintain and develop academically as well as in school. Will you be familiar enough with the programme in a local school to support your children as they progress? How much homework will there be, and can you give them the help that they will need to complete it?

How Important Is the Social Aspect of School?

This isn't just something to consider for your child, it's something to consider for yourself too. Most, if not all, of your potential new friends can be found at the school gate and some schools have a strong parent social scene with well organised and well attended events, coffee mornings and trips. On the other hand, others do not so it's worth asking about if it's something that's important to you.

Age of Your Child

Consider if you will be moving in the future at a crucial time of their education; GCSE year in England, Wales and Northern Ireland, for example. Disrupting education then may be problematic, so look far ahead.

At one point during our expat life, we calculated that our eventual move back to the UK would coincide with when our daughter would be due to enter the two-year GCSE exam preparation. Having spoken to quite a few schools in the UK I discovered that *not one* of them would accept her at this critical point in the school system. Her very limited choices would have been to drop back a year or two or find an online school or home educate to get her through those vital exam years. It pays to keep up-to-date with your options at fundamental educational stages and to keep an eye on the future. Thankfully it has all worked out well for us, due to pure luck, a different educational year and some judicious reorganisation of our entire lives; but it could have been very difficult for us all.

If you have more than one child, it should hopefully be easier to get them into the same school. But that isn't always possible, so this is something else to consider when making your decision.

Another point to note is the different mandatory school starting ages in other countries. It can be quite a shock for a child who started school in the UK at four or five years old to move to a country where compulsory education doesn't start until they are seven years old. Going 'back' into a kindergarten setting can be quite disturbing for some children.

Does the School Day Fit in With Your Lifestyle?

In some countries, the school day starts and finishes early. Very early! Our school in South Africa started at 0730hrs and ended at 1400hrs or earlier. And the school run often took nearly an hour. Too early for us, but we had to do it as it was normal there. Not quite so normal, was this particular school would be 'cancelled' for the afternoon with notice only being emailed at 1700hrs the day before. The cultural expectation was that mothers do not work and are always available for school runs.

If you will be working this may cause difficulties. It is worth checking that the school's hours fit around your working life or any other commitments you may have to avoid mayhem for your career (and sleeping pattern!).

Countries also differ in the structure of their school day and the length of their school holidays. To cite just a few examples: in Australia, the school day is typically 0900 – 1530hrs. In Brazil and Germany, a typical school day is 0700 – 1230hrs, with children home by lunchtime. In China, however, a typical school day is 0800 – 1700hrs, with a two-hour lunch break! This can be particularly challenging if both parents work.

As for school holidays, I couldn't possibly list the differences between every country here. Some have very long summer breaks with little to no other holidays in between, while others spread their breaks more evenly throughout the year. And of course, summer in the Northern Hemisphere isn't the same as summer in the Southern Hemisphere!

To give you an example of what I mean in practice; in South Africa, the main school holidays are during the Southern Hemisphere's summer – through November, December and part of January.

The school year and main intake starts in January rather than September as in the UK. But the American school carried on with their Northern Hemisphere timetable, so their holidays are through June, July and August, with their new school year starting in August. Confused yet?

The school our daughter attended in Pretoria used the South African school year dates, January to December, which actually worked out well for us with our return to the UK. It's enough to give you a headache, but it's worth knowing these matters in advance.

How Far Away From Your Home Is the School?

Would you be able to get to the school quickly and easily in case of an emergency? You may also want to consider the distance between home and school affecting your children's ability to socialise with their friends outside of school and whether not being able to see their friends may lead them to becoming unhappy.

How Will the School Run Work?

Some countries have school buses, others do not. If you aren't planning on driving in your new country either to begin with, or at all, you'll need to consider how easy it will be to make the journey back and forth on public transport.

How Does the School 'Feel'?

Get a feel for the atmosphere in the school. This isn't something you can get from the internet and will require a visit or two.

You can ask any number of questions but ultimately one of the strongest indications of whether the school is a good fit will come from your gut. You should get a feel for the atmosphere in the school and have an idea of how comfortable your child would be there. Do remember though – your child is not you. The sort of school you would have enjoyed attending isn't necessarily the same as the one your child will fit into best.

Don't limit a child to your own learning, for he was born in another time.
Rabindranath Tagore

Research Your Options

There are so many things to take into consideration when choosing your new school, you may feel like you're only just scratching the surface when researching the different options and making the relevant considerations. Nevertheless, it's an important part of the process.

With everything available at the touch of a button the internet is the obvious place to start. It is worth your internet research being taken with a pinch of salt though. School websites naturally place an incredibly positive spin on their school.

Speak to colleagues, other parents and anyone who has a connection to the country you're moving to. The expat community is rich with experience so speak to colleagues, other parents and anyone who has a connection to the country you're moving to and the schools that you're interested in.

Visit the School

If possible, have a selection of schools to choose from and if you can visit your new host country prior to your move, contact each one and make an appointment to visit them to help you decide which one is best for your family.

It's a good idea to chat to the students – and if the school tries to keep you away from them, consider what they might be trying to hide. Ask them what they like about school, what their favourite lessons are, who they go to if they need help. If they're enthusiastic and engaged, it generally means the teaching is enthusiastic and engaging too. On the flip side, if the answers are vague and they seem uninterested it may be worth digging a little deeper and even reconsidering your choice.

Questions to Ask the School

Go with a list of your questions and prioritise them in order of importance to you and your child. The following list will give you some ideas to get you started, although it's good to bear in mind that each school is different, and your requirements may be more specific.

Admissions Criteria

- Is there a place available for my child? If not, how long is the waiting list and when would they realistically be able to start?
- Are there any admissions tests?
- Is there a policy to admit siblings?
- What is the nationality and diversity of their students?
- Does the school advocate and work hard towards inclusivity?

Education

- How many children are in each class? And how many per year group?
- What is the teacher to pupil ratio?
- How are students streamed for ability?
- How is diversity of ability dealt with in the class room, at both ends of the spectrum?
- Are measures in place to assist those with special educational needs and those who are gifted and talented?
- What is the staff turnover at the school like?
- How much homework can be expected?
- What subjects, sciences and languages are offered as exams in the later school years?
- What focus is there on life skills?

- How is religious education taught, if at all? Does this align with your beliefs and wishes?
- What incentives, rewards and discipline systems are in place?
- What do they do if you have a student who is smart but is not performing?
- How do they identify students who need extra help?
- What do they do if a student isn't coping with the workload?
- How do you help a student who is struggling?
- Where do the students go after leaving this school? Is further education facilitated by the school?

Pastoral Care

- How often do parents meet with teachers?
- What contact methods are there between school and parents?
- How do they help new children settle in?
- What do I do if I have a concern about my child?
- What are the mobile phone, internet and social networking policies at school?
- Are parents involved immediately in issues such as bullying, behaviour or other problems?
- How does the school handle bullying? If any staff member says there is no bullying, be suspicious. Either they are lying, or they are unaware due to failures in the anti-bullying system.

Extra-curricular Activities

- Which sports are available and where do they take place?
- What extra music tuition is available? Where and when is it held?

- What other activities are available? Lots of extra-curricular activities indicate that teachers are enthusiastic and prepared to put in an effort.
- Are the extra-curricular activities free, or do they have to be paid for?
- Are there regular school trips?

Facilities

- Are the buildings and facilities in good condition?
- Do students need to leave school grounds for any activities such as sports? If yes, how is this handled?

Extra Expenses
- What resources do the school provide and what resources are parents expected to pay for?
- Who pays for extra help if your child has special educational needs?

These questions are also repeated at the end of this book, so you can find them again easily.

FIVE POINTS TO CONSIDER BEFORE CHOOSING A SCHOOL OVERSEAS

The big picture doesn't just come from distance; it also comes from time.
Simon Sinek

So, at what stage are you in your plans to relocate abroad? Are you thinking about it? Are you already in the throes of moving?

The fact that you're reading this guide means you have a decision to make in common with the rest of us expats and frankly, it's probably one of the toughest decisions you'll ever have to face.

HOW TO CHOOSE A SUITABLE SCHOOL OVERSEAS?

You'll agonise over the choice, or lack of it; whether your child will be happy and make friends; whether the education will be as good as it is back home and whether they'll learn the language. You'll also have to contend with pesky little dilemmas, such as when is it best to move given their school start dates and a 'settling into a new home' period.

In our case, it was back in 2006 when we first knew we'd be moving to Japan. Our daughter was due to start school in September – the typical start of term in the UK – but we knew we'd be moving to Japan at the end of November.

The dilemma was, should we let her start school in the UK knowing she'd leave in less than a term, or should we keep her at home until January 2007 when her new school in Japan would accept her?

We decided to let her start school in the UK. She loved that she was a 'big girl' starting school in her smart new uniform. As things turned out, the school wasn't a particularly good one and we were left wishing we hadn't bothered, but at least I had some child-free time to pack up and get ready for our move!

Thankfully, her experience of school in Japan a few months later was nothing short of amazing and she did academically well the whole time we were there.

There's no right or wrong answer when you're faced with situations like this and you won't be able to anticipate everything that may crop up.

What you can be certain of, is that choosing a school is rarely a matter of simply finding the best of the best among its academic bunch or league.

For starters, it's wise to look behind the scenes to, for example, determine how well the school deals with bullying; whether the teachers are happy (in other words, how good is the Head); and whether the children are well behaved.

There's also whether your child will flourish there socially; if the school has provisions for children with special educational needs; if it has extra-curricular activities to broaden their talents all-round, and so on.

The sum of these factors and more, help you determine whether the school is well equipped to help your child develop multi-dimensional skills throughout their school life and beyond. In other words, there's more to choosing a school than academia. It's an entire journey, where they can meet new friends, soak up new experiences and learn valuable skills for life.

The challenge is, of course, the vast distance – literally oceans – between your home and host country, which makes it difficult to visit schools before you arrive.

I can't emphasise enough how much of an impact your relocation abroad will have on your child. It's incredibly important to research as much as possible, so that you can make a well-informed decision before you thrust them into an unfamiliar environment.

Your research initially might be limited to the internet, which is perfectly fine. Nowadays, most schools have a website, from which you can download a prospectus. This will give you an overview of the school's location, size, curriculum, ethos, enrolment requirements and past exam results. All a good starting point to get the ball rolling with your enquiries.

Do bear in mind, however, that each school is trying to sell itself, so its own marketing information will inevitably paint a positive spin on everything. Carry out supplementary research by asking other expats for recommendations or speak with anyone who has a connection to the country, and if possible, specifically with a school you are considering, so they can give you an insider's view.

Visit forums and chat rooms, such as my own Expatability Chat Group on Facebook. You'll meet expats who have had similar experiences in selecting schools overseas. They'll be only too willing to give you helpful advice on specific countries.

If possible, have a selection of schools to choose from. This will obviously be dependent on the country you're relocating to. Just as an example, international schools are usually situated in the city centres, so if you're staying anywhere other than there, you might be limited to whatever is available.

Give yourself time to carry out as much research as possible. I didn't realise before it was too late that our first choice of school in Berlin had only nine children to a year group. Yes, the *entire year* – incredibly small! And they had all clearly started school together since the start of their formal education, which meant they'd formed their own little cliques. As you can imagine, it was difficult for an 'outsider' to form new friendships.

Remember, you are choosing for *your* child. What may seem right for other parents and their child, may not be appropriate for you and yours.

At times, you need to step back and look at the bigger picture.

To help make that decision a little easier for you, the following are five points I believe every parent should consider before choosing a school overseas. I mentioned these before, but they are so important that I want to go through them again with you:

1. **The length of stay in your host country**
2. **The age of your child**
3. **Any language preferences**
4. **Lifestyle and culture**
5. **Special educational needs**

In the next section, I give an overview of why you should consider these five points; a recommended school option (or options) which may be most suitable; the relevant chapter to read on the recommended school; and a plan of action for you to do some homework, i.e. research.

The chapters on each school option make up the bulk of the guide. I've designed it so that you can read it from cover to cover, or alternatively, dip in to which ever chapter you feel is most suitable given your family's circumstances and the needs of your child.

Whichever way you decide to use this, you'll find there's lots to take away. The recommendations are based on challenges I and other expats have experienced in choosing a school overseas, so you can be confident that you're not alone in making a similar decision.

LENGTH OF STAY

One of the first things to consider is whether you intend to stay permanently, or whether you'll move on elsewhere in the future (and if so, where?). While many children are resilient and adjust well to moving schools, the impact of the change in routine, surroundings and curriculum can still prove challenging.

We knew we would be moving on from Japan after our mandatory four year posting there, but we were fully expecting to return to the UK. I spent months searching for suitable schools in the UK, only to end up having to find a school quickly in Berlin once our posting was unexpectedly changed!

Of course, last minute changes are part of expat life – you clearly won't be able to anticipate and plan for everything that may or may not happen. But by thinking ahead, for example whether you'll be staying one year, four years or a dozen years before repatriating, you can decide whether to choose a school that runs a similar curriculum to one that is run in your home country. This will make it easier for your child to transition back into the curriculum when you return home.

If, however, you intend to move on to another country, as we did, consider choosing a school that offers the International Baccalaureate® (IB)[9]. The beauty of this scheme is that IB schools follow the same curriculum at the same time throughout the school year. In theory, this means mobile/expat children won't miss out on any subjects wherever they move.

If you intend to stay permanently, it will make more sense to consider a local school, as this will allow your child to become fully immersed in the local language and culture.

Don't be afraid to change schools if your first choice turns out to be the wrong one. We had to change schools in Germany and in South Africa too.

Recommended Chapters

Staying permanently? Refer to chapters on '*Local School*'; page 89, and '*Learning the Host Language*'; page 161.

Staying one to four years? Refer to chapter on '*International School*'; page 69, and Home Schooling; page 109.

Homework

If you're moving elsewhere, or repatriating soon after, check if the curricula are similar or find out whether the IB is available.

AGE OF YOUR CHILD

Firstly, be aware that the age at which children start their formal education (literacy and numeracy) differs throughout the world.

In the UK, this starts at five years of age and in some cases, as early as four, while in other parts of Europe, formal education won't start until they're seven or eight. If you have a child around this age and if they've already started their formal education, they will seem to fall behind slightly. My advice is not to become overly concerned about it. Children catch up again quickly at this young age.

When it comes to settling in, younger children seem to be more adaptable to change than older children, who may have already settled into a school system elsewhere. With kindergarten or primary-aged children, you're probably more interested in getting them into the school spirit and in helping them to look forward to learning in a fun environment.

For older children who are already settled into a school system, your main concern will be whether they'll adapt to moving between different curricula. It's often difficult to judge how well they'll cope until they're attending their new school. It might simply be in their best interest to continue with what they are used to and then change when they seem settled.

If you have more than one child and would like them to attend the same school, check whether the school has a sibling policy to avoid any unpleasant last-minute surprises.

Do consider whether you will be moving at a crucial time of your child's education, such as during their exams. This can be particularly stressful for teens who are naturally concerned about their further education or career prospects. Do all you can to minimise disruption for them at this delicate time.

Older teens and young adults are obviously of an age where they make their own decision regarding the University they want to attend. But you can still play a valuable role in helping them with their research.

Recommended Chapters

If you have toddlers or pre-school children – see chapter on *'Kindergarten'; page 99.*

Primary or secondary children – see chapters on *'International School'; page 69, 'Local School'; page 89, 'Home Schooling'; page 109,* and *'Online School'; page 115.*

Teens/young adults – see chapter on *'Boarding School'; page 119,* and *'University'; page 131.*

Homework

Remember to check terms and holiday dates, as they differ per country.

Don't forget to make a note of crucial dates such as exams, SATS, etc. to minimise the stress of moving during these times.

LIFESTYLE AND CULTURE

Think about your lifestyle, i.e., the country or city you're moving to, your commitments, where you'll live, whether you will be working, how you'll get about etc. The school you're considering should fit in seamlessly around your normal routine.

For example, if your career requires you to travel frequently, boarding school may be the best option for your child, as at least they'll be settled in one place while you travel. You can still have weekend and holidays for visits. However, if you're staying permanently, you can clearly take your time getting used to your new lifestyle, in which case a local school might be more suitable.

A popular choice for expats is an international school, as they suit people who are moving on within a few years. They're a melting pot of cultures and nationalities, so an excellent choice for parents who want their children to experience diversity around them and make friends from around the world while they travel.

Of course, there's also the ordinary day-to-day and how you'll manage that too. For example, how will you cope with the morning and afternoon school runs? If you have a car and are willing to play taxi of mum and dad, that's all well and good, but if not, you'll have to factor in getting to grips with the local public transport – if there is any. How will you manage the practicalities of getting back to school in case of an emergency, or letting them socialise with their friends after school?

In Tokyo, the school our daughter attended had a hideous school run of two and a half hours *each way* by metro, including nearly two miles of walking. This was not fun with a tired five-year-old. Once I worked out how the buses operated this journey was much more comfortable but was still almost an hour's journey door-to-door. Then we bought a car and the school runs were managed much more efficiently and quickly.

In Berlin, as is usual in our personal circumstances, we had no choice where we could live. Also, we couldn't go on a preliminary visit, so the school was chosen completely online. Bear in mind, at the time of choosing a school, we had no clue where we would live. The school we chose quickly and online only, turned out to be 20km from our home! Thankfully, the school had a bus service to take care of school runs each way. Unfortunately, other, major problems arose with that school, so we did have to move her, and the new school was much closer.

In Pretoria, there is no public transport to speak of, and the school my daughter attended did not have its own transport. So, I was back to doing school runs at difficult hours of the day.

Trust me, factors like these have a bearing on whether life in your host country runs smoothly, or whether it's a disruptive and stressful mess for the whole family.

Similarly, cultural differences seem quaint when you're learning about them in the comfort of your own home. But once you're abroad, they take some getting used to, especially for your child in the context of their school day.

Will there be religious ceremonies? Do they differ from your own faith, if you have one? Will your child be required to attend them or is attendance optional? It's something to think about if the cultural or religious differences in your host country are very different to your own.

A cultural difference I wasn't expecting in South Africa is the necessity of someone being constantly available for drop off and pick up during the exam period (usually a couple of months, twice a year). Your child is *only* allowed to be in school for the duration of the exam and needs to leave as soon as the exam has finished. When an exam is only an hour long, this makes for a frustrating day. It's well known, locally, that mothers here are basically home-bound for the exam seasons. And yes, it *is* generally the mothers…

COSTS

Do factor in costs too, as not all education overseas is free of charge – even with government funded schools. Check if the school you're considering has tuition fees and whether you can afford them for the duration of your child's stay there.

You may also need to pay for school items, such as textbooks and stationery. In the U.K., these items are usually provided by the school, but that's not necessarily the case overseas and can prove to be a surprise if you only discover this on the first day of school. Germany – I'm looking at you here!

We're used to children wearing school uniform in the UK, so when we moved to Japan, we weren't surprised to learn that we'd have to buy uniform there too. What we *didn't* expect was a change in school uniform every year. We also had to purchase summer clothes, winter clothes, indoor shoes and outdoor shoes. We could only purchase them from one store – via mail-order and based in the States – and the store never had enough stock. Very odd.

However, many country's schools don't have a school uniform at all, so you may need to decide how this will work for you. I found it easier when my daughter was younger to have a 'pretend' uniform of, say jeans and a set of t-shirts, rather than a morning panic. Now she's older, pretty much anything goes, and this works well for such an individual teen!

If you'd much rather experience the lifestyle and culture at a much slower pace without the confines of a structured school day, home-schooling may be more suitable for you. It takes your child's education to a whole new level, where you can teach as creatively as you please in the way your child likes to learn. You do need to be aware however, that home-schooling is prohibited in some countries, so do check whether this applies to the country you're moving to.

Recommended Chapters

'International School'; page 69, 'Local School'; page 89, 'Home Schooling'; page 109, 'Online Schools'; page 115, 'Boarding School'; page 119.

Homework

Check distance between home and school; if you don't have transport, check public transport links or whether the school has a bus service.

Check whether there are additional fees for school (e.g. uniform, text books, etc.)

LANGUAGE CONSIDERATIONS

If you travel because of your career (or you're a travelling partner, like me), my guess is you have little choice where your posting takes you. I know only too well what that means – learn the language, pronto!

If, however, you travel at will, then you clearly have more choice over what language you'll learn. Or, perhaps you're already raising children in a multilingual family and are fortunate enough to have a posting in the country of your mother tongue.

Whatever your reason for learning the host language, it's clearly an important consideration, as you naturally want the whole family to be able to communicate effectively. If anything, it's vital for your child in their new school, as they'll likely spend more time at school than they will at home.

The good news is, children pick up learning a new language much quicker than adults, so you can prepare them by helping them learn before they move. How fluent they become, however, will depend on how much they're immersed in it.

If you want your child to be fully immersed in the language, one option is to send them to the local school where they'll obviously spend their school day with local children.

Sending them to a local school is not without its challenges, as one of my interviewees, Mary Johnson discovered. There are also unique challenges in ensuring a child of a multilingual family retains their second or third language, and even in keeping up with their English.

Be aware that international schools generally teach lessons in English. While they may offer some additional support to assist in learning the local language, opportunities for your child to become might be limited to additional language lessons you can organise yourself.

Recommended Chapters

For schools: *'International School'; page 69, 'Local School'; page 89.*

For languages: *'Learning the Host Language'; page 161, 'Raising a Bilingual Child'; page 173, Mary's Johnson's Interview, 'Why we Chose Full Immersion'; page 169, and 'Keeping up With English in a Foreign Country'; page 177.*

Homework

Check whether the school can provide additional support with learning the local language.

SPECIAL EDUCATIONAL NEEDS

If you have a child with special educational needs, you'll already be aware of just how important it is to plan meticulously, so that you can create as smooth a transition as possible for them.

Local (i.e. state/government) schools are obliged by law to provide support for children of all needs. In this regard, they might be marginally better equipped to support children with special needs than International schools, where the focus is on attracting the money. That's not to say International schools don't provide SEN support. Some do, but you may find support patchy and inconsistent.

There are obvious challenges in sending a child with special educational needs to a local school, where they'll be fully immersed in an unfamiliar environment, language and cultural setting. This clearly requires careful consideration.

It should also be noted that some countries are woefully lacking in suitable SEN support at school, so you will need to carefully research beforehand to determine what facilities are available in the country and city you are moving to. You may simply need to garner suitable support by talking to individual teachers on a case by case basis.

And finally, there is of course the option of home-schooling, if it's permitted in the country you're visiting.

Recommended Chapters

Check out, *'Special Educational Needs'; page 139, 'Home Schooling'; page 109, 'Online school'; page 115.*

Homework

Get any documentation required to support your child's needs.

YOUR CHILD'S HAPPINESS

Self-esteem is the real magic wand that can form a child's future. A child's self-esteem affects every area of her existence, from friends she chooses, to how well she does academically in school, to what kind of job she gets, to even the person she chooses to marry.
Stephanie Martson

I snuck this one in, because it's an important note to end this section on. Ultimately, your child's happiness is the most important consideration of all.

It really isn't the end of the world if the school you originally choose isn't a so-called perfect fit. You can change your mind if it's not working out and you shouldn't be afraid to do so. Changing schools won't ruin their life. I know this is something every expat parent fears, but I promise you, it won't. Your child will adapt.

If you have the luxury of moving overseas first and looking for a school while you settle, this is obviously the best option of all, as you can then involve your child in the search and choose one they fall in love with.

But if it's not an option, simply do your best at becoming super sleuth. Talk to other expat parents and find out as much as you can before you move. Choosing the right school doesn't have to mean choosing the best school. Remember the bigger picture and keep an open mind.

What's more important, is finding something that best meets the individual needs of your child, while ensuring they will be happy and well settled in your host country.

IN DETAIL: SCHOOL OPTIONS OVERSEAS

Education is the passport to the future, for tomorrow belongs to those who prepare for it today.
Malcom X

I've established there are highs and lows to raising your child overseas and that there's a bigger picture to choosing a suitable school – it's not just about academia.

I've explained Expat Child Syndrome and promptly filed it to one side just in case of need.

And I've highlighted five things I think all parents should consider before choosing a school abroad.

Let's now consider each school option in more detail:

- International School
- Local (National) School
- Kindergarten
- Home-school

- Online or Virtual School
- Boarding School
- University
- Special Educational Needs

In each case, I've presented popular reasons expats choose these options (benefits), further tips on how to get the best out of them, and potential challenges.

I've also included a selection of responses from my ExpatChild Survey, conducted among 200+ expat families[10]. I think you will find their responses thought provoking and particularly helpful if you can relate to similar challenges.

For the sake of completeness, I've included University, as it's common nowadays for older teens and young adults to pursue their further education abroad.

So, if you're ready, let's dive in.

INTERNATIONAL SCHOOL

An international school is a school that promotes international education, in an international environment, either by adopting a curriculum such as that of the International Baccalaureate, Edexcel or Cambridge International Examinations, or by following a national curriculum different from that of the school's country.
Wikipedia

For those who want their children to mix with a diverse group and attain a more internationally recognised set of qualifications, international schools may be the best option.

International schools are often hailed as the best education option for expats, as they equip our children with a comprehensive education as well as opportunities they would not have found at local schools.

International schools will usually ensure that students are taught in their first language, and because of the fee-paying nature, the curriculum is often richer and more appealing than a local school would be.

In most cases, lessons in international schools are taught in one language (predominantly English). For children from English-speaking countries, this can be less of a culture shock. For expats from non-English-speaking countries, a good command of colloquial English might help them in future. English has become the language of global media and business, with many international universities teaching courses in English. English is a widespread and globally spoken language. It is a transferrable skill and for children from non-English speaking countries, their opportunities will be expanded by being able to speak good English. It will also help them develop contacts and have a common ground language with their peers at school.

International schools usually also teach at least one other language – the native language of the country you're living in. So, in Japan, your child will receive Japanese lessons; in the UAE, Arabic lessons are the norm and so on. Often many other language lessons will be available in a single school, such as French, Spanish, Mandarin and many more. This does depend on the school though, so it is worth checking whether the international school in question provides language tuition to your children.

If you're likely to move on in a few years, or need a certain curriculum, an international school may be the best option for your child.

However, there are many things to consider, as with any aspect of relocating to a new country. Here are some of the main features of international schools and what to expect.

DIFFERENT TYPES OF INTERNATIONAL SCHOOLS; BEATING THE CONFUSION

Before you made up your mind to move overseas, I'm willing to bet that it hadn't crossed your mind there were so many different types of school to choose from, let alone so many types of international school?

What is an International School?

Let's start with the basics, which many of you will already know, although, this is a bit of a loaded question because of the diverse nature of the schools we're trying to lump together.

An international school is an educational facility for children, usually up to age eighteen, that operates outside of the normal state system in any given country. Originally set up for the children of expatriates – mainly families of embassy staff, international businesses, armed forces and missionaries – these schools teach an international curriculum such as the IB (International Baccalaureate). They often have international values reflected in their mission statements and their teaching ethos. These schools are populated by multinational and multilingual pupils and staff, many of whom come and go during the school year as the expat life can be transient, to say the least.

The idea is that for those children who are on the move around the globe, international schools provide a form of stability; their values and teaching will be similar wherever you are in the world and it's easier to transition from one international school to another, than it is to go through a wide range of local education provisions. A lovely idea – but due to the growing variety of international schools, many of which now accept local as well as international students – it doesn't always work like that and you must choose very carefully.

Let's Talk About the International Baccalaureate®

If you know you will move countries throughout your child's educational years, one way to avoid the curriculum changes is to choose a school that runs the International Baccalaureate® (IB) programme which was created as a solution to this issue. It caters for the potential for repeating, or missing subjects by having a fairly global timetable.

The International Baccalaureate does have a different teaching methodology from other curricula which can prove difficult to switch to if your child is coming from a more classic, or country-based, national curriculum, so make sure you research thoroughly to see how you can help your child adapt. In simple terms, the methodology encourages pupils to learn how to learn and to do much of the work under their own steam. This is diametrically opposite the more traditional style of teaching and learning of providing a prescriptive and directed education. Some children work well with this and others do not.

International Baccalaureate schools were built in recognition that as a greater number of families took to travelling, there was a need for an aligned and standardised curriculum to make it easier for their children to learn effectively. There are currently around 3000 IB schools across 245 countries, educating over a million international children between the ages of three and nineteen.

The IB curriculum is rigorously academic and achievement based and is crafted to give international children a head-start on acceptance into Universities. Teaching staff must be IB accredited and there are strict acceptance criteria for children, but also there is little doubt that this is widely considered to be the gold standard of international education and well worth considering.

I should also comment on the fact that a true International Baccalaureate education starts from a very young age. This is something that many people are surprised to learn as they are often only aware of the IB Diploma. In the UK, for example, the International Baccalaureate is mostly recognised as a more senior education, and as an alternative to A levels.

Further to my comment above about the differing teaching and learning methodologies, I believe that the earlier your child can enter the IB programme, the easier it is for them to 'learn how to learn' this method. Moving from a traditional learning style at a later age may prove too much for them to make a success of it, particularly if the teachers aren't understanding of this difference.

From the age of three to around eleven or twelve years old, children can attend the PYP – Primary Years Program – which "focuses on the development of the whole child as an inquirer, both in the classroom & the world outside". Then pupils aged eleven to sixteen years move on to the Middle Years Programme – MYP – which "encourages students to become critical and reflective thinkers". Finally, the students work towards the IB Diploma Programme which is an "academically challenging and balanced programme with final examinations that prepares students for success at university and life".

It should be noted, however, that some countries (the UK for example) still don't have many fully IB schools, and those that do exist are London based. So, if this is an educational programme you're interested in, make sure your future destinations can provide what you need.

British, American and Canadian Schools

These international schools are in a category sometimes referred to as 'original expatriate', meaning that most pupils and staff (as well as the teaching curriculum) are from the one country of origin. This might be the best choice for a child who is expatriating for a short-term period with a foreseeable plan to return to their homeland or elsewhere with similar school options, because they will be learning roughly the same curriculum content at roughly the same ages.

I say 'roughly' for a reason – it's worth checking out what relationship each of these schools has with their native country. Some are very closely linked, with staff offered exchange opportunities and the same Senior Management Team and Governing Body – but some have drifted rather further away and receive no support or endorsement from the native governments.

The British schools show the greatest diversity in this respect with some of them teaching almost nothing of the current British curriculum. To keep as close as possible to the original idea, look for schools that are members of COBIS (Council of British International Schools); many apply but only the best few are granted status.

Other International Schools

Other countries are well represented in the international school arena too. In most places you will find a German international school, or Deutsche Schule and French international schools which are usually referred to as the Lycée.

International Group Schools

As the name suggests, these are groups of schools that all share the same management structure, curriculum, assessment method and values. A child could transfer quite easily from one school to another in the same group, even if they were in very different locations. Examples of group schools are...

- GEMS – teaching roughly 142,000 students across 16 countries and committed to four core values that are integral in each of their schools regardless of location.
- Nord Anglia – perhaps the largest group with 56 schools around the world including the US, Asia, Europe and the Middle East.
- Cognita – fast growing, with schools so far in eight different countries.

[Figures correct at the time of going to press]

'Broadly International' Schools

These tend to have a curriculum that is broadly (and loosely) modified from one country but accept children and teaching staff from all over the globe. Instruction is almost always in English, but the curriculum is tweaked to suit a huge ethnic diversity. These are perhaps the most international schools of all the categories out there and well suited to families of a very nomadic nature.

Local International or Bilingual Schools

This is the largest and fastest growing of the international school types. These are local schools, serving a local populace, yet also encourage international students. Their curriculum tends towards approximating that of the host country, but heavily modified to include a quota of the subjects delivered in English. These schools, despite the

English language in many lessons, are considered immersive in nature; the overall language, culture and format is that of the host country.

BENEFITS OF AN INTERNATIONAL SCHOOL

Like-Minded Expat Community

International schools are a popular choice among expats, because they offer a varied international curriculum, either through the International Baccalaureate Diploma (IB), Edexcel[11] or Cambridge International[12] exams.

Here's the International Baccalaureate's mission statement:

"To develop inquiring, knowledgeable and caring young people who help to create a better and more peaceful world through intercultural understanding and respect..." and "to develop challenging programmes of international education and rigorous assessment. These programmes encourage students across the world to become active, compassionate and lifelong learners who understand that other people, with their differences, can also be right."

It's an ethos that attracts expats who naturally want their children to be enriched by an environment of diverse nationalities and cultures wherever they travel. International students feel at home when they're in a community of like-minded individuals and schools are usually well equipped to welcome newcomers on a rolling basis throughout the year, to help them feel welcome whenever they join.

Farah*, who attended an international school in Dubai, loved the opportunity to take the IB and meet students from different countries.

"It was a terrific opportunity to meet people from all over the world. I was also able to attain a qualification that is accepted in any country I decide to settle in."

Farah has gone on to attend a university in the UK and has kept her global contacts from her international school days.

Name changed to protect privacy

A Broad and Diverse Curriculum

In addition to the International Baccalaureate, many offer the option of the English GCSE and 'A' Level curriculum, the American High School Diploma and College entrance exams, and other national qualifications depending on the type of international school attended, e.g. if represented by a specific country.

An example of this type of school is a French international school, where the staff are French, pupils are French, and the curriculum is French. Many countries are represented in this way, so you'll similarly see schools abroad that are British, German, Japanese, American, Canadian, etc.

Other than the obvious cultural appeal if you're a native of the country the school represents, the benefit of attending one of these schools is that in addition to being able to study the IB, your child will have the opportunity to study a core national curriculum, leading to a relevant diploma or degree of that country. So, for example, a French International school will offer a choice of *"diplôme national du brevet"*, the French *"Baccalauréat"*, the *"Option Internationale du Baccalauréat"* (OIB), or in some cases all three.

Similarly, bilingual schools offer a bilingual education – teaching in both English and the local language – and will usually follow the national curriculum, leading to a national qualification. The benefit of attending one of these schools, is full immersion in the language while being able to retain English.

As Farah found, students who study in an international setting find that their studies better equip them for an international career in later life, which let's face it, nowadays extend across international borders.

A Blend of Cultural Academic Experiences

Lessons are taught predominantly in English. This naturally has an appeal for parents of students from English-speaking countries, as they can focus on settling into the school environment without the challenge of learning the language to communicate at school. Non-English-speaking students have the obvious advantage of attaining a higher standard of English, which will benefit them going forward if they decide to pursue a university education internationally.

Despite their Westernised approach, an international school will still have its own character, shaped by the local culture, its teachers, students or even parents. For example, In Tokyo, we had 'Japanese Days' where all the students and teachers would dress up in something traditionally Japanese. We had people dressed in Kimono, Japanese school uniform, Sumo wrestlers, etc., They spent the day working on traditional crafts and made typical Japanese food. It was great fun and made a unique and special culture more accessible and immersive.

While a local school may suit children who will be in the country for several years or permanently, truly international schools are probably the better option for those who move around frequently. If your first language is English, or if your child has ambitions to work internationally, the education in

English will ensure that they have a good basis for business, education and socialising.

CHALLENGES OF AN INTERNATIONAL SCHOOL

As English is spoken throughout the school, your child may not have enough opportunity to learn the host language.

International schools often do offer support in learning the local language, plus a choice of other languages too (especially at secondary/high school level), but these lessons may not be enough to become fluent. In cases like this, you may need to organise additional language tuition privately.

However, it's important to note that not all international schools are as international as you may hope, or as they encourage you to believe. My daughter attended a couple of self-titled international schools that were treated as elite schools for rich, local families. The pupils were nearly all natives of that country and, because of this, spoke their language at any opportunity and actively excluded foreign pupils whose language skills weren't up to native level.

I can't emphasise enough that it pays to do your research. Contact other expats via forums[13] to discuss the positive or negative aspects of the schools you're considering. School inspections or grades can only tell you so much; the real experiences of children at school and the opportunities available to them are a much better indicator of how suitable the school really is.

~~~~~

WHY WE CHOSE AN INTERNATIONAL SCHOOL

ExpatChild Survey: Clara Wiggins

Clara is a British mother of two. Her children have been educated in Pakistan and St Lucia – preschool; and UK and South Africa.

How did you make the education choice for your child(ren)?

We researched available schools and narrowed it down to two. We were then lucky enough to be able to visit each school. We based our decision on the quality of education, facilities, how happy the children seemed and security. I followed up with a long Skype meeting with the school counsellor before we made our final decision.

Would you have done anything differently? Is there anything you wish you had known before making this choice?

We researched thoroughly so, I don't think there is anything we would have done differently.

Why did you decide to choose an international school?

We chose the international school for several reasons:

1. Because the school year was closely aligned to the school year from our home country.

2. Because we liked the school and believed the educational quality would be better than the available local schools for their age group.

3. Because I wanted the children to mix with many different nationalities.

How did your child(ren) cope with the transition from school back at home (or elsewhere), to international school in your host country?

My eldest daughter coped excellently. As the school has a high turnover, they are used to welcoming new children and helping them integrate successfully into the school. She is very sporty and really appreciated the sporting opportunities on offer.

She did however find the work very easy and early testing showed she was far above grade average. We had pointed this out to be a probability before we started, but I think they only took us seriously after the testing. They then tried to differentiate her work more than they already had been – with partial success.

We had similar issues with my younger daughter, but she didn't settle in as well. She had a very small class size and I think found it hard to make friends in her first year with the choice that she had. Her second year seems to have been a happier one

Did you choose to follow a specific curriculum? If yes, which?

No – if we had the choice, we would have chosen the UK curriculum at this stage. Or if the UK followed the IB we would have chosen that.

What do your children love most about attending an international school?

Probably the sports and the emphasis on the creative – so being able to learn an instrument, lots of arts and Spanish, etc.

What tips would you give to other parents considering an international school?

Depending on what system you are coming from, try and find out as much as possible about their academic side. If necessary, consider getting a home tutor to top up. I think they will gain more from the school community and the experience of mixing with people from different cultures than they may lose on the academics.

~~~~~

WHY WE CHOSE AN INTERNATIONAL SCHOOL

ExpatChild Survey: Zara

Zara* is an American mother of two, whose children started elementary school in San Diego, California. The family moved to Barcelona, expecting to stay a couple of years but they ended up spending eight. Here's her experience:

How did you make the education choice for your child(ren)?

When we first moved abroad from the USA to Spain, our primary criteria was an American-accredited elementary school, so that they would get credit for any work they completed overseas. Then we looked for a community with a nice mix of locals and expats, realising that a mixed community would be more tolerant and welcoming to transient families.

Would you have done anything differently? Is there anything you wish you had known before making this choice?

Nope! We have been in two international schools in Barcelona, Spain. I continue to believe that it is important to have a mix of locals and expats, particularly if there is a language barrier or if you are only overseas for a shorter period. Long-term families and locals don't always want to make friends with "One and Done" families, so you need a mix to have a social life!

Why did you decide to choose an international school?

I chose an international school because I wanted my children to meet friends from all over the world. They have been at two schools in Barcelona, both with a rough mix of $1/3$ American, $1/3$ Spanish local and $1/3$ International. I love the fact that when my kids look at a globe, they recognise countries by the friends they know from there (or who have moved back to there) and the places to which they have travelled!

How did your child(ren) cope with the transition from school back at home (or elsewhere), to international school in your host country?

My kids coped very well, but they were young at the time (eight and ten). They barely spoke any Spanish when we arrived, so they didn't grow as close to the kids who spoke Spanish/Catalan in the playground. But we were lucky that English was the common language for the diverse European crowd, so they quickly made friends from children from other parts of the world.

What tips would you give to other parents considering an international school

FYI, some of my advice is directed at the subset of international parents who are looking at sabbaticals. Namely, they can choose the country, city, school and length of stay.

Look for a school with a vibrant community for the parents, as well as an enriching academic program for the kids. When you move abroad, the parents at your school will become your family. We've been lucky to have two schools with amazing planning for parents – city tours, language classes, welcome committees, neighbourhood parties and WhatsApp groups offering advice and help.

Our new families are thrilled to be here, comfortable from the first month and you'd be surprised how many end up staying years longer than they originally planned. In contrast, we have known a few families who moved to Spain for a sabbatical and placed their kids in a local school so that they would be immersed in Spanish. But if you as a parent don't speak the local language, you will be very limited in your participation with the school or community. It's easier to be isolated as a parent, even if your kids are learning a lot. Most of the time, those families leave after a year (or even less).

Understand the programming, goals and limitations of your new school. There are some international schools with amazing facilities and academics that rival the best

American prep schools. On the other hand, there are other international schools, particularly outside of capital cities, that don't quite make it to that upper echelon. I think it is super important for parents to really understand what a school can offer their student, and then consider whether that school will serve the needs of their student.

For example, remember English probably isn't the home language for most the students. If $2/3$ of the student body is essentially English-language learners, the English literature programs might move more slowly than you are used to. I've had friends who cringe when they realise that a friend's child in 10th grade Honors English has read three novels (plus Beowulf) in the time their kid's class is slowly dissecting some work of Young Adult Fiction.

I've spoken to friends who came from huge A+ rated public schools in American university towns, who explain that when their child finished "Discrete Math" at high school, they took classes at the university. Well, when those parents hit our small school in Barcelona, they are horrified to learn that we have 10th Grade Math standard or high level – and the local colleges speak Catalan so taking classes there isn't an option.

I've known other parents who came to our school (which is well respected by the locals for its success in English-immersion) and immediately pitched a fit that there wasn't more tuition in Spanish so that their kid wasn't bilingual within the year.

Others, who have come with elementary, middle or even high schoolers, don't seem to realise that Spain doesn't play lacrosse or American football until they get here! They then spend their time freaking out that they need to hire private coaches, otherwise their kid won't make the team when they return Stateside.

It's the mistake some parents make of assuming international schools can match what their kids are used to back home – without considering things like variations in size, cost, or even purpose. In my experience, a small international school cannot offer the depth and breadth of a large high school or an elite prep school back home in America.

If it is critical to you or your child that they stay on a very accelerated high school academic track, or that they play a specific sport on a level equal to or above their home team, I would suggest you reconsider your move, or choose your school very wisely. Otherwise, you are fighting an uphill battle.

Please take advantage of everything the school DOES offer and embrace your time away from your home culture. Rather than lament the fact that you can't take Calculus BC as a sophomore, take a class on dancing the Sevillana. Learn Spanish and cooking at the same time, by taking local classes at the Market. Travel Europe with your schools MUN or Debate Team. Try all the unique things you can do in the new culture, instead of asking the school to replicate what you had back home.

What do your own children love most about attending an international school?

They love having friends from all over the world. December 31st was' amazing because New Year's

Greetings came in through Snapchat throughout the day from almost every continent.

My older daughter has gained such an amazing perspective on current events, simply by chatting with friends who fled Libya during the Civil War or working side by side with Brits the day after the Brexit vote.

And of course, they love the travel – MUN conferences in Lisbon, Soccer in Geneva, Debate in Prague.

Do you have any other comments about your overseas education experiences?

You bet I do!

Please encourage families to get involved with their international schools. An international school has a community like no other, but that spirit depends on *you*.

Every year, new families are welcomed, and old families leave. Traditions survive, and amazing events happen because new people get involved every year. Your experiences abroad will be so much richer if you take the time to volunteer for events. Just remember, the events you enjoy can't and won't happen without volunteers.

I always got frustrated with moms who came for a year and would tell me they were super busy in their home city and didn't want to do anything here. No one owes you a bespoke international school experience, complete with book clubs, International Food Day and cocktail parties. So, join a committee, lend a hand and, for goodness sake, host a book club. You'll be happy that you did.

Remember that your perspective is your perspective, but it isn't necessarily the right one or the prevailing one. One of the biggest PTA battles emerged my second year over the school lunch. American moms were packing an apple, juice and sandwich so their kids could gobble it down in five minutes and go out to play, while the Spanish moms wanted a three-course hot meal to be eaten in silence over 30+ minutes so their kids got their main meal.

Until you really start working with people in another culture, you won't recognise some of the cultural differences. From sandwiches to fundraising, another culture has a very different point of view. So, get involved and be open to understanding, "Is this really important to you? Can you tell me why?"

Name changed to protect privacy

LOCAL SCHOOL

State school – In the United Kingdom, the term 'state school' refers to government-funded schools which provide education free of charge to pupils. There are also non-government schools, called private schools.

In the United Kingdom, most schools are publicly funded and known as state schools or maintained schools in which tuition is provided free. There are also private schools or independent schools that charge fees. Some of the most selective and expensive private schools are known as public schools, a usage that can be confusing to speakers of North American English. In North American usage, a public school is one that is publicly funded or run.
Wikipedia

WHAT DO *I* MEAN BY 'LOCAL SCHOOL'?

As you can see from the description above, there could be many interpretations to this.

Very simply put, I mean *not* an international school as described in the previous chapter!

Local (national government-funded schools) primarily serve local families who were born and brought up in the local area. It will follow the curriculum, language and culture of that country.

Ideally suited for those of you moving on a long term or permanent basis, or if the language and culture is something you are all familiar with. Don't forget that as parents you will need to be able to understand the language used at the school in order to fully help your child! An English-speaking family moving permanently to Australia, for example, will be particularly compatible with choosing a local school for their children. In this case, even if they're moving for a couple of years, a local school will work well. An English-speaking family moving to China for a couple of years would be advised to consider a different educational option.

In some countries, you may find a local school that also teaches in English – a bilingual school – or will certainly take steps to accommodate a non-native speaker, so it's worth checking these out too.

Pick a school that is close to where you live to ensure your child gets to mix with the local children outside of the playground too, and that they have the opportunity to build friendships as they go.

BENEFITS OF LOCAL SCHOOLING

Integration Into the Local Language and Culture

An obvious advantage to sending your child to a local school, is that they will be attending with children from the local area, an excellent way to fully immerse them in the local language and culture. But of course, preparation is key. If you're going to send them to the local school, learn as much of the language as possible together before you move. Even simple greetings or phrases will help.

Carmen Maidment from the UK, now living in Dordogne, opted for a local school for her two children as it's the closest to the family home.

> "With the benefit of hindsight, we would have had more language tuition before coming. The children coped well with the transition from school back home. It was a little difficult at first, but six months on, they're nearly fluent."

Her advice to other parents considering a local school?

> "Just go for it, kids adapt super-fast, although adults less so!"

Some schools offer classes and extra assistance to help English speaking students learn the language while they're at school and nowadays, there are handy apps or online resources you can utilise to help you learn together. These can help make learning a new language fun, but don't underestimate the level of work involved in your child learning a new language, it can be both challenging and tiring.

We expats often get a bad reputation for refusing to socialise with the local community.[14] It's tempting to rationalise, from an expat's point of view, that it's easier to stick with expat friends, especially if the culture is very different to your own. But refusing to integrate only puts up unnecessary barriers. Not helpful if you intend to stay in that country permanently.

Some countries run international exchange programmes in collaboration with participating schools, offering young people the opportunity to travel to a new country and experience the culture while sharing their own as an ambassador for their home country.

These exchange programmes are usually designed for children between twelve to eighteen years of age, and they will stay with a host family from anything between one to six weeks.

Obviously, it does mean that your child would be away from home for a while, which requires careful consideration, but it could be a fun way for them to explore your new host country before you relocate, and it could mean a gentler settling in.[15]

CHALLENGES OF THE LOCAL SCHOOL CHOICE

Difference in School Starting Ages

As I've already mentioned, children start their formal education at different ages throughout the world.

If you have a child around four or five years old who has already started their formal education in the UK, for example, and you're moving to a school where they will effectively start over again, you will need to prepare for the possibility that they will fall behind slightly. In this I mean, they may fall behind the progress you may expect if you'd stayed in your home country.

In general, children catch up quickly at this stage, but I appreciate it's a thorny subject if your child is extremely bright and already ahead of their peers. It's especially noticeable if your child has recently moved to 'big school', with a smart new uniform and a book bag, then moves countries to attend a school in 'kindergarten' or nursery mode.

There's no one-size-fits-all solution to this problem. You may simply need to keep an eye on the situation and if necessary, provide supplementary tuition or talk to teachers to see whether there's a possibility of your child skipping a year. I should warn you that skipping years doesn't happen as often as you may believe. The Head is unlikely to agree to this until they're entirely satisfied your child is familiar with the curriculum and fluent in the language.

If you find yourself in this situation, simply try to take it in your stride. Your child has enough to cope with settling into a new school, learning a new language, getting to grips with a new curriculum and of course making new friends. And they certainly don't need academic pressure at this stage of their lives! You can always fill in the blanks at home if you wish.

Term or Semester Differences

In the UK and the rest of the Northern Hemisphere, we're used to our set term times of September to June/July, or Mid-August for American schools. Moving to a country (e.g. in the Southern Hemisphere) where this routine is different can take some adjusting to.

Children usually adapt as it's only a slight change in routine, but it can mean they end up working ahead of their peers back home. This was the case with my daughter in the South African school she attended where she ended up taking her GCSE exams six months ahead of her peers in the UK.

Incidentally, the system in South Africa – and some other countries too – is that a child must 'pass the year' i.e. make the grade in order to move up a year. Some students in the school were twenty years old. This was not necessarily because they failed to make the grade but; some had, but others had moved from another school and wanted to do 'A' levels to go on to university in the UK.

If you notice your child is falling behind, or they're put into a lower class where they find the work simplistic and unchallenging, if possible, see if you can liaise with the school Head to provide additional support where necessary.

Curriculum

Local schools will naturally follow the national curriculum and lessons will be taught in the local language. Of course, if the local langue is the same as yours, it's much less of an issue. However, if there's a whole new language to learn, research your options very carefully. While it may be one of the best ways to learn the local language and culture, it means completely immersing your child into entirely unfamiliar territory. It's a lot for them to take in, so be mindful that it can make their day a tiring and potentially stressful one.

Language immersion is only part of this: your child will also be learning mathematics, history and other subjects in another language. It's a huge amount for them to take on.

I mentioned earlier that I believe you shouldn't be afraid to move your child from one school to another, if the school turns out to be unsuitable for your child.

The happiness of your child is far more important than saving face, so don't hesitate to make prompt changes if you feel it's the right thing to do.

~~~~~

WHY WE CHOSE A LOCAL SCHOOL

ExpatChild Survey: Ange Keskey

How did you make the education choice for your child(ren)?

We wanted our family to be immersed in the culture. For us that means schooling, language skills and living in a neighbourhood with a host-nation influence.

Would you have done anything differently? Is there anything you wish you had known before making this choice?

We are pleased and still confident after nine months. Both of our kids are learning German in German schools. The key was knowing our kids and trusting the schools and ourselves to be able to support them through the hard times. But with the benefit of hindsight, we would have started more concentrated tutoring before we left home.

Why did you choose a local school?

Language skills are increasingly becoming more valuable in the US. It has amazed us to hear our neighbour's pre-teen kids speaking three – four languages. We wanted to give that gift to our kids. In our opinion, it's an essential part of the culture.

How did your child(ren) cope with the transition from school back at home (or elsewhere), to school in your host country?

The first few months were hard. Four hours a day listening to a language you don't know is insane, but total immersion has developed an age-appropriate level of conversational German that amazes us. We chose to hold our eight-year-old back a year, so that the school material wouldn't be new and so she could concentrate on language. Friends have been tricky but manageable. The school staff has been amazing.

What tips would you give parents considering a local school/full immersion?

Do it! Give your kids an opportunity of a lifetime. But have a backup (e.g. an international school) if things are just too hard. Our kids are more resilient and more adaptable than we give them credit for. I have heard other parents say they are doing an international school for the first year to help with the transition, then they will go to the public system. The problem with that is they will make friends in that year and won't want to be 'the new kid' again.

~~~~~

WHY WE DECIDED AGAINST LOCAL SCHOOL

ExpatChild Survey: Imogen Gorman

Imogen Gorman's children were educated in the UK and Argentina. Her honest response on what can potentially go wrong when choosing a local school shows there's another side to the coin which you may need to consider.

How did you make the education choice for your child(ren)?

Initially we chose a local school based upon the notion that by sending our children to a 'local' school, they (and we) would have a more 'authentic' experience. It didn't exactly turn out that way. It wasn't all bad, but when we switched to the American international school, life was just much easier.

Would you have done anything differently? Is there anything you wish you had known before making this choice?

I wish I had known that sending my children to the school where the majority of the expat community choose, makes life easier. It may not be the 'best' school, but you are among a community that understands your experiences in a way that a 'settled' community does not (however wonderful they may be). With the benefit of hindsight, we would have started in the American/International system.

What tips would you give parents considering a local school/full immersion?

Think very carefully. Is this for you or for your child? Yes, they may pick up the language and get a local experience, but they are not 'a local child' and may be sensitive to their 'difference' when compared to their peers. Conversely, when choosing the 'expat' school, also ask yourself the same question! In my experience, children don't just 'fit in' (to any system), it is more complex than that.

They may need to leave behind certain characteristics that makes them the person they are to fit in and may have to take on new characteristics. This may make them adaptable, but they need to maintain a strong sense of 'self' to remain resilient in the face of potentially several moves throughout their childhood. An expat identity is sometimes easier to maintain within the international school system. Perhaps the advice is 'tread carefully' with this choice. It's not necessarily a bad choice and can be an amazing one, but it takes hard work and extra effort in my experience. We (eventually) chose the International school as the local school didn't work out.

What do your children love most about attending an international school?

They loved the variety of languages, the richness of cultures, the fun, the sense of community and of being part of 'something' (or was that me). They went in with big smiles on their faces and came out the same way.

KINDERGARTEN, PRE-SCHOOL
AND NURSERY

Kindergarten: (in Britain and Australia) an establishment where children below the age of compulsory education play and learn; a nursery school. (In North America) a class or school that prepares children, usually five- or six-year-olds, for the first year of formal education.

Pre-school: A nursery school.

Nursery: A place where young children are cared for during the working day; a nursery school.
Oxford English Dictionary

First of all, let me explain my interchangeable words here – in effect, kindergarten, pre-school and nursery all mean generally the same thing; somewhere a child goes before they reach compulsory school age. Because different words are used by different people and different nationalities, I have taken the liberty to muddle them about a bit. Sorry! I hope this doesn't confuse you.

In more detailed terms, nursery, or nursery school, can also be referred to as child-care or day-care. Often a place for little ones from birth to three or five years of age, depending on the environment.

Pre-schools aim to prepare children for the school years. They're usually for children between the ages of three and five years old. Often a pre-school may be attached to a primary school. Not necessarily physically attached, but there may be an associated school the children move on to when they reach that age.

In some countries, kindergarten is the first stage of a child's formal schooling and is mandatory at a certain age. However, in other countries, it's simply another word used for a nursery.

Which is why I, personally, use these words interchangeably!

Rather than semantics, what is more important is to look at the goals, philosophies, teaching methods, and more, of any pre-school and decide which is a good fit for your child. There are several teaching approaches at this stage of education too, such as Montessori, play-based, and academic preschools.

Local Language or Bilingual?

Moving abroad with toddlers or pre-school-age children is so much easier than moving abroad with older children or teenagers who will already have social groups they won't want to move away from. In fact, I'd say this is the ideal age to move overseas with children.

Will you choose a kindergarten in the local language, or go for a bilingual option which may be available in your location? Bilingual nurseries aren't particularly common, but you'll most likely find them in places where there are large expat communities.

BENEFITS OF A HOST-LANGUAGE PRE-SCHOOL

An Early Transition Into Local Language and Culture

At this stage, finding a pre-school sooner rather than later will give them a better chance of making a seamless transition into the local culture, as well as into the education system. After all, social and educational choices made in the early years are as crucial as those made at primary and secondary level. These are all-important foundation years, when you want to instil in your child independence, confidence and a willingness to learn. Immersing them early on will go a long way to helping them achieve this.

Jill Hodges'[16] daughter attended kindergarten in Italy. She said the experience helped both her and her daughter.

"Kindergarten is a great time to make local (non-expat) friends and for children to get foreign language exposure. I made a lot of friends myself through the local kindergarten."

I can relate to this. School gates of any kind are usually a great place to meet new friends.

Sending your little ones to a local kindergarten also happens to be an excellent way of helping them learn social and emotional skills that they might not otherwise be exposed to.

Here's what American expat, Kari Martindale[17] had to say about sending her daughter to a German Kindergarten.

"Sending my daughter to German Kindergarten opened her eyes to a different social dynamic. Teachers allowed children to work things out on their own, instead of forcing them to share for example, or separating them when they were arguing.

Teachers were much more hands-off than we were accustomed to seeing. While our daughter was learning to handle the system, we too had to restrain our own instinct to intervene, as typical American parents.

We had to accept that children could go into the school yard to play on the swing-set without supervision, so long as they told a teacher.

We became less protective as we noticed that our five-year-old was capable of more than we'd thought. I joke: German Kindergarten teachers would not intervene unless someone's eye was actually being poked out with a stick, and even then, only to clean up the eye, put it back in the child's head, and tell them to soldier on."

Kindergartens and pre-schools tend to be generally similar around the world, generally offering play-based learning to children between three to six years old but be prepared to have a good search for one that you'll like.

Developing countries such as India and parts of Africa may face challenges in providing good facilities due to harsher economic conditions, and in China, for example, kindergartens will tend to be found in the more developed cities than rural regions.

POSSIBLE CHALLENGES

Play-based Learning Until at Least Aged Five

I must admit that I don't really consider this to be a difficulty, but I've included it here because if you're a parent of a five or six-year-old moving *from* the UK, the chances are your child will have already started in a more formalised education setting, and learning reading, writing and simple arithmetic.

As I've mentioned before, it may come as a surprise to you if you relocate to one of the countries where children of this age at kindergarten are only engaged in play-based learning. In my opinion, there's no need to panic or become unduly worried about this. Here's why I say so, plus the research to back it up.

There have been many campaigns calling for a change to the start of formal education here in the UK (e.g. the 'Too Much, Too Soon' campaign).

Cambridge University researcher, David Whitebread, one of the signatories to the "Too Much, Too Soon" campaign, explained what the psychological and developmental research shows, in relation to the contribution of playful experiences to a child's development as learners, as well as the consequences of starting formal education at the age of four or five.

"... studies have also consistently demonstrated the superior learning and motivation arising from playful, as opposed to instructional, approaches to learning in children. Pretence play supports children's early development of symbolic representational skills, including those of literacy, more powerfully than direct instruction. Physical, constructional and social play supports children in developing their skills of intellectual and emotional 'self-regulation', skills which have been shown to be crucial in early learning and development. Perhaps most worrying, a number of studies have documented the loss of play opportunities for children over the second half of the 20th century and demonstrated a clear link with increased indicators of stress and mental health problems."

While there is a possibility your four/five/six-year old child may seem to 'fall behind' when they start a different school overseas, it's unlikely to do any lasting harm at all.

Whitehead goes on to explain:

"Studies have compared groups of children in New Zealand who started formal literacy lessons at ages five and seven. Their results show that the early introduction of formal learning approaches to literacy does not improve children's reading development, and may be damaging. By the age of eleven there was no difference in reading ability level between the two groups, but the children who started at five developed less positive attitudes to reading, and showed poorer text comprehension than those children who had started later. In a separate study of reading achievement in fifteen-year olds across 55 countries, researchers showed that there was no significant association between reading achievement and school entry age."

You should, however, take note that the standard of teaching in kindergartens overseas varies and might not be as high as you are used to, or even to your liking.

In a report on "Early Childhood Education and Care in Dubai", by Dr. John Bennett of the University of London, it was found that although 90% of children were enrolled in kindergartens before compulsory schooling, at minimal cost to the government (many privately owned), 70.3% of Emirati children were enrolled in kindergartens where it was deemed the quality of services were variable or showing room for improvement.[18]

International kindergartens are frequently found in countries with large expat communities. However, enrolling your toddler/pre-schooler into a local, monolingual nursery, rather than an international one, can be hugely beneficial for their language skills. Friends of ours in Tokyo, both British, enrolled their baby into a local nursery as they both had to work. The baby's first words were in Japanese and caused many double takes when they were both out and about as a family!

WHAT TO CONSIDER WHEN CHOOSING A KINDERGARTEN

Do ask for a viewing, preferably during a normal day, so you can see the structure of daily activities for yourself.

- Visit the premises and meet the staff, rather than relying on brochures or reviews.
- Try to choose one that is local, or at least within walking distance from your home. The fresh air while walking to school will act as a calming, morning routine and will help your child's concentration levels for the rest of the day. And even better, calms them on the return journey home too.
- Check outdoor facilities (climbing frames, hammocks, stepping stones, etc.) to discover how many hours a day

the kindergarten provides children with space to explore and develop their vital, gross motor skills.

- Ask whether there is bilingual or multi-lingual support, where the national language and your family's native language differs.

- Talk to other parents and ask advice – you'll meet them when you take your little ones to a recreation ground, park, shops and so on. Don't be shy! It's important for you to feel confident about where your child will be spending time.

If you have any doubts that they're not getting on well in their new kindergarten, find another one promptly so you can re-settle them as quickly and as smoothly as possible.

~~~~~

WHY WE CHOSE A LOCAL KINDERGARTEN

ExpatChild Survey: Stine Posselt

How did you make the education choice for your child(ren)?

My kids started their education at an international school (preschool/nursery) in China. At the time, I found it the easy choice as all staff spoke English and tuition was paid by my husband's workplace.

We moved to the US a year ago and decided to put our kids in a public school. We want our kids to 'fit in' and to have their school friends close by. The choice here seemed easier as our kids speak English and the public schools in our area are very good.

Would you have done anything differently? Is there anything you wish you had known before making this choice?

I am very happy with our choice. My only one 'regret' is that my two boys had to start pre-school as soon as we got here. The school clearly wasn't prepared for two boys who had just moved from across the other side of the world and had some adjustment issues. We moved them to another school after about 3 weeks, and they were very happy there.

What do you think were the main benefits of sending your child to a local kindergarten?

They get the same education as the locals and get a chance to learn how to navigate in their new country in a way, I think international schools don't give them.

What tips would you give other parents who are considering sending their child to kindergarten overseas?

Don't forget to consider public schools. They are not as scary as you might think, and I find the staff very supportive and helpful with the few issues we have had with being 'foreigners'.

Do you have any other comments about your overseas education experiences?

Speak up! Ask questions! Don't be afraid to say: "I am new to all of this, what does this and that mean?"

HOME SCHOOLING

Home schooling, also known as home education is the education of children at home or a variety of other places. Home education is usually conducted by a parent or tutor or online teacher.
Wikipedia

Some parents choose to home educate their children when they move away, either for personal reasons or because of the high fees at international schools.

Home educating children in a foreign country can be amazing, because it allows you all time together to explore the culture and environment you find yourselves in.

Expats who home-school do so because it means flexibility around travel. They're free to study the local culture at leisure and of course, there's no need to worry about adapting to a new school environment.

BENEFITS OF HOME EDUCATION

Freedom and Creativity

Home schooling also suits families with children of with special needs, as those needs might not be suitably met by a traditional school. In some instances, it might be the only option, if there's a lack of suitable schools in the country you're relocating to.

In general, it can offer a child a consistency and stability that is hard to achieve if you're moving from one school to another, in different countries and time zones.

Dan*, who spent his childhood in Singapore, remembers how the expat community at his school had a very high turnover rate.

"Every month or so, my friends from other countries would leave and move elsewhere."

*Name changed to protect privacy

Despite the term home-schooling, however, it really shouldn't be thought of as school at home. The beauty of this type of education, is that it allows you to be as creative with your teaching as you please.

On this, The UK Education Act 1996 states that it is the parent's duty to:

"Cause (the child) to receive efficient full-time education suitable to his (or her) age, ability and aptitude and to any special educational needs he (or she) may have either by regular attendance at school or 'otherwise'."

The law doesn't define what it means by 'efficient' or 'suitable', but states that "education is 'efficient' if it achieves what it sets out to achieve and 'suitable' if it prepares the child for life in the society to which they belong". It should also allow the child to achieve their full potential.

Additionally, the Department of Education and Health in the UK takes the view that a child's education should provide for their "physical, intellectual, social, spiritual and emotional development."

As a home-schooling parent, what you provide at home clearly doesn't need be the same as provided at school to achieve the above. If anything, you probably have more flexibility.

For one thing, it means you can tailor your teaching around the needs of your child, while giving them one-on-one attention. If, for example, they learn at a slower pace, you can take your time in reinforcing their learning, or find alternative ways to do so. This is rarely possible in traditional schools, where teachers must balance the needs of the many against the needs of the few—typical class sizes in the UK can range from anything between 20-30+ pupils.

It also means you can be more hands-on in your approach to what you're teaching. Compare a traditional geography lesson from the confines of a stuffy classroom, to a field trip in the local countryside, where you can spend the day (or even a few days) exploring the 'classroom' outside. In fact, your relocation abroad can be a live geography lesson. Yes, schools do organise field trips from time to time, but as a home-schooler, you can weave these into the very fabric of your family's daily life.

There is, of course, the advantage of being able to travel when you need to while not having to uproot your child from school in the process.

Joanna, one of the participants of my online survey, home-schooled her children in the UK and continued when they moved to the Saudi Arabia.

She cites the best part of home-schooling while travelling as,

> "Having more flexibility with regards to term dates, being able to study the local culture in depth, and having more time to explore."

The downside for her, was that not many older children were home-schooled in the Middle East. However, her children were still able to enjoy pursuing their hobbies and passions. They also took advantage of the wide variety of online resources available nowadays, such as Khan Academy[19] and Conquer Maths.[20]

Of course, there's nothing stopping you from hiring a tutor to help your child benefit from a different teaching style, or to teach a subject you might not be able to teach yourself – another language for example. Thanks to the internet, online tutoring makes it possible to access private tuition wherever you're located. Kings Tutors[21], for example, operates Skype tuition online, and there are many more depending on your requirements.

Home-schooling doesn't mean there isn't a routine. Many home-schoolers have a routine that their children are used to, such as set days for indoor lessons and set days for field trips; or alternatively for younger children, some find that early morning lessons with late morning play works best.

Mix Home-Schooling With Traditional Education

Many parents successfully blend early years home-schooling, with traditional high school or further education.

Simply be guided by your needs as an expat and the needs of your child. It's an experience you can share with other expats and one way to make life-long connections. If a network for home-schooling expats and children doesn't already exist, why not set one up yourself (if the country you're vising permits it)? Advertise on expat forums, social media and notice boards in the relevant locality to get the word out. It will not only help your child, it will help you too. The support and friendship will undoubtedly enrich your experience of settling into your new host country.

CHALLENGES OF HOME SCHOOLING

Prohibited in Certain Countries

In the UK, if your child receives what the government calls a 'full-time education' at home, you don't have to follow the National Curriculum, but as each country differs check to ensure you comply with the regulations of the country you're relocating to.

What surprises many people is that there are countries where home-schooling is restricted or even illegal. Unexpected examples of this are, Germany, Netherlands, Costa Rica, and Sweden.[22] Parents who felt strongly about wanting to home-school, have no option but to move on to another country.

For a comprehensive list of the legal status of home-schooling throughout the world, please see Endnotes and Resources at the end of this book.[23] You can also contact the Embassy in your home country for more information, if this is available to you.

A Full-Time Job

If home-schooling is not something you are already familiar with, you will need to weigh up whether you have the energy for it, as it is very hands on. It is a full-time job, so you should carefully balance your child's education with your work and travel commitments. How will you feasibly fit it in, while ensuring they benefit from a broad and varied spectrum?

Requires a Carefully Planned Curriculum

You can't (and shouldn't) view it as something you can make-up as you go along. While home-schooling is flexible, and you have license to be far more creative in the way you teach your child, you should still have a plan and a carefully thought out curriculum.

This might be particularly challenging if the country you're travelling to insists you follow its national curriculum. You may also find that your child must sit exams to obtain qualifications that can be transferred to other countries. You wouldn't want to jeopardise their chances of getting into their dream university because their education was incompatible with the application requirements.

Home-schooling can also be expensive. You'll need to foot the bill for all your textbooks, stationery, additional tutors (if required) and examinations for their qualifications. Having said that, many schools require you to pay for these anyway!

You will also need to balance home-schooling with finding plenty of social activities, so that your child doesn't feel isolated. Some children flourish at home alone, while others feel they're missing out on making new friends, having a social life and experiencing the culture.

ONLINE SCHOOLS

An online school (virtual school or e-school or cyber-school) teaches students entirely or primarily online or through the internet.
Wikipedia

A different form of home schooling is attending an online, or virtual, school.

An online school brings the entire school experience – teachers, curriculum, learning materials and classmates – to your family wherever you are in the world. The best virtual schools are fully accredited for serving students around the globe and offer engagingly rigorous academic programs that deliver students to the world's top universities.

A VIRTUAL EDUCATION

Because virtual schools operate via technology, they can adapt very quickly to the kinds of urgent circumstances expat families sometimes face. Many expat parents find themselves in situations like these:

- You've been offered the promotion of a lifetime – and the only hitch is that your family will need to move overseas next week.
- You've identified the perfect international school for your child, but you're 50th on the waiting list and the first day of school is just around the corner.
- You're relocating in the middle of the school year, or relocating for a short-term assignment, or both.
- Your child is so anxious about being uprooted from their regular routines that they're acting out in class – and your new school abroad has asked you to place them elsewhere, immediately.

Using digital technology, virtual classrooms form the basis for teaching on the web. These classrooms are just like physical ones, a teacher is present via a webcam, a whiteboard area is used to deliver the lesson and students can input and interact through a microphone device and keyboard.

The digital aspect of school means each lesson can be recorded and stored, so if a student has been ill or away and needs to catch up, or simply wants to go over old lessons to prepare for exams and tests they can access them as if they were in the lesson again.

BENEFITS OF AN ONLINE SCHOOL

Special Educational Needs Provision

The actual structure of an online school benefits children with special educational needs greatly. Accessing school from a comfortable setting such as the students home not only makes them feel at ease with contributing in lessons, it removes the distractions and disruptions of a traditional classroom setting, further improving the child's education.

Another issue that many students face is having anxiety in asking the teacher for help when they do not understand a particular question or topic. The ability to have one-to-one conversation with the teacher in the middle of lesson reduces this anxiety attached to asking for help, resulting in the student leaving the lesson with a thorough understanding of what's been covered.

DRAWBACKS TO AN ONLINE EDUCATION

Because a virtual school is entirely reliant on technology, it won't be accessible if you live somewhere there is no competent internet connection or reliable electricity.

Lack of Recognition

To date, the only country to officially recognise the existence of online schools is New Zealand. Many other countries class online education as a form of home schooling which means it is therefore legal as an alternative form for mandatory education. In years to come, it is highly likely that further countries will follow and officially recognise online schools as a genuine form of schooling.

Your child can be educated to exam level, but you will need to arrange and pay for them to sit these exams as an individual. A good online school will advise you further on this.

A couple of excellent online schools are the International Connections Academy[24] which is a global virtual school. They prepare students for college or university via online, individual courses and summer schools. And InterHigh[25] is the UK's biggest online school with over 1000 students from around the world, 30% of which study from outside of the UK. The school has been used by many British expat families that want their children to study an accredited British education.

BOARDING SCHOOL

A boarding school provides education for pupils who live on the premises, as opposed to a day school.
Wikipedia

Most expat parents dream of finding their children a good school, local to your home, which provides the academic and pastoral support your child needs. But sometimes this does not happen. Or perhaps your expat career means you move every year or two, which is generally not a great life for children. Being the 'new kid' at school is stressful and can be difficult for children to deal with too often. Sometimes, a boarding school back in your home country – or even elsewhere – is a more appropriate choice.

Being apart from your children is one of the taboos of modern life. And you may well feel judged by people who don't understand that you are doing the best for your children. It is a difficult decision for most parents. I cried for days when we made the decision and that was prompted by our daughter's request!

Boarding school life is actually great fun for teenagers who get to experience many activities and a life they wouldn't normally get elsewhere. The Harry Potter books and modern St Trinian's films have inspired children and many are excited and keen to experience the fun and excitement of boarding school, even if it isn't Hogwarts.

BENEFITS OF BOARDING SCHOOL

Continuity of Education

A boarding school provides a continuity of education, one curriculum through the years and stability in a safe environment.

Moving from one country to another, one school to another, one language to another, one curriculum to another plays havoc with a child's education.

Yes, I know I'm advocating moving abroad with your children, and yes, it's an amazing life experience for them. But, and I'm being honest here, moving frequently can prove detrimental to their education and it gets harder for them as they become teenagers.

Ideal for Stability

If you move frequently, or move to countries where the schooling isn't great, or to countries where day-to-day life may be unsafe or difficult, a boarding school can provide the stability and smooth education your child needs.

Expats who travel frequently because of their career (e.g. military families, etc.) should opt for a 'full boarding' school, as it provides a child a degree of stability.

A full boarding school means most weekends are spent at the school, often with lessons on a Saturday morning and games/sports fixtures in the afternoon. Full boarding schools are becoming quite rare these days as they relax their rules to encourage more local families to join.

Nowadays, boarding schools tend to offer flexi-arrangements, with a mixture of weekly or even day boarding, where children spend the day at school and go home late at night. Alternatively, they will have arrangements where they spend a night or two boarding, for example, if it's a specialist school such as a music or choral one.

Many will have superb activities over the weekend, such as sports matches, concerts and plays – and of course nowadays, technology means that no child is truly cut off without any access to the outside world. In any case, true full-boarding schools, where no-one leaves at the weekend, are quite rare.

Weekly boarders stay at school from Monday to Friday and leave the school at the weekend, or every other weekend. While this isn't perfect for overseas parents, it may work well if you have a reliable relative or guardian near the school.

The location of the school is vitally important if you travel frequently outside the country. In our case, we were lucky to find an excellent boarding school near the airport. You'll find it much easier to manage if you have friends or family in the area who can help with school holidays and short breaks.

There is also a growing trend for UK boarding schools to open satellite campuses overseas. These have the advantage of being linked to an historic, traditional boarding school in the UK, while following a UK curriculum overseas. A link to a full list of these schools is included on the Resources Page.[26]

An Environment That Nurtures Independence

Our daughter spent two and a half years at a wonderful preparatory boarding school in the UK, when she was between eleven and thirteen years of age and she loved it.

It meant a degree of independence away from us (which tween doesn't want that?) and it meant she experienced extra-curricular activities and trips she wouldn't otherwise have had access to, such as regular theatre trips to London and sailing in the English Channel.

Even though the school was in the UK, her fellow pupils, and the ones she naturally gravitated to, were mainly from expat families and other TCKs. Her best friends were Spanish and Russian and English – and she keeps in contact with them to this day, often visiting the school so she can catch up with her friends and teachers.

For her, boarding school was a very positive experience and can be for your child too – especially if your career requires you to travel frequently. It's possibly more favourable to putting them through a long string of local or international schools wherever you travel.

Excellent Facilities

Boarding schools provide an excellent array of extra-curricular activities and sports. As for the 'right type' of boarding school, some are sporty, others are academic, and others focus more on the arts. My suggestion is you seek a school that will enable your child to flourish, given their personality, talents and strengths.

CHALLENGES OF A BOARDING SCHOOL

You Need a Reliable Guardian

It is a legal requirement for students in the UK whose parents live abroad, to have a UK-based guardian. This is usually someone over the age of 25 (although some schools will insist on someone older), who can represent the child *in loco parentis* for emergencies or parent/teacher meetings, and generally help monitor their social and academic development.

A good guardian will also become a surrogate parent to your child and will hopefully take them out at weekends, whether it's for their birthdays and even just for a fun break from school life. So, you'll obviously need to consider who you can entrust to support your child in this manner, not least because they will need someone they can quickly turn to for help or advice if you're not available.

I cannot emphasise enough that a trustworthy, caring and reliable guardian is absolutely essential for your child's well-being while at boarding school. The lack of a reliable guardian will be detrimental to your child who is living away from their parents, so take this into consideration as a priority. This was the main reason my daughter couldn't continue to attend boarding school in the UK and meant she had to move to South Africa with us; and so, the school search started all over again!

Most boarding schools have at least one mandatory holiday each half term, usually called *'exeats'*, which means 'a leave of absence' and all pupils will be expected to leave the school over this weekend. This will also need to be carefully planned with your guardian to arrange suitable care in your absence.

Lengthy Registration

The decision to send your child off boarding school is not an easy one and the process of getting into your chosen school can be a long, drawn out one. If you are seriously considering a boarding school, I highly recommend you allow at least two years to plan, allowing for registration cut-off dates and selection exams. Bear in mind there's often powerful competition for the more popular schools, which quickly become over-subscribed.

Potential Boredom at Weekends

If the school is *not* full-boarding, there may not be many children who stay in the school over the weekend. It's not unheard of for some dormitories to be empty at the weekend. If your child has nowhere to go, this can be lonely or distressing for them.

Published boarding figures may not tell the true story about how many children stay in the school over the weekend, so you'll need to ask this question directly when you visit and ask everyone you meet at that school, including the other pupils.

Do also find out whether children who full board are within your child's year group, and preferably the same gender, so your child can make viable, strong friendships.

QUESTIONS TO ASK WHEN VISITING A BOARDING SCHOOL

Once you've researched the schools thoroughly, you will, of course, need to visit them. Here's a list of typical questions that often arise, which may help you decide whether the boarding school is suitable for your child.

(N.B. Tommy Cookson, Daily Telegraph Education Expert also gives some excellent tips for getting the most out of boarding school open days in his Daily Telegraph Article, "Boarding School, How Does It Work." [27])

Is the School a Member of a Regulatory Body or Association?

A good boarding school will be a member of a reputable governing body or association, such as the Independent Schools Council (ISC)[28] and The Boarding Schools Association[29] for the UK. And there are others depending on which country you're considering.

Academic

- What are the class sizes? (The appeal of boarding school is the individual attention teachers can give each child. The smaller the class size, the more attention they will receive).

- Additionally, how does each class handle different abilities?

- If your child has talents or strengths (e.g. sports, art, music, science, etc.) how will these be met?

- How well has the school performed in past academic results?

- Which universities do pupils go on to after leaving this school? (While league tables provide a quick and simple method to compare one school with another, they are only part of the overall picture of how well the school helps its pupils reach their full potential).

International Pupils

- What provisions does the school make for international pupils?

- Does the school organise transport to/from train stations/airports? If not, how close is public transport to the school and how long/complicated is the journey to the airport.

- Is there one person at school who is responsible for them?

- Is the school flexible about when the pupils leave / return to fit in with flights? This is vital if you live somewhere where there is only one flight a day, a problem we experienced. The only flight out of the UK departed at 2100hrs, but school finished at midday on the last day of term – so, what to do to kill time between then? The return flight landed in the UK at 0600hrs, meaning some dedicated soul had to be up early to meet her at the airport. She was often too exhausted to learn on that first day of school. There are dedicated concierge services – such as Airport Angels[30] – who can provide meet and greet and care of your child at the airport, so perhaps investigate this to help you all out.

- Which social events / meetings are international parents expected to attend and how much notice does the school give?

- How are parents' evenings and important informational meetings dealt with for expat parents? Our school would live stream their presentations, so overseas parents could watch. Amazing foresight.

Weekends

- What percentage of students are day pupils or full boarders?

- How many boarders stay at school during weekends?

- What activities does the school organise for weekends? (Ask to see a typical program of events)

- How much free time do pupils have? How do they normally spend this free time?
- Does the school offer social events with other houses / schools?
- Does the school facilitate expat boarders to stay for an exeat with boarders from the school who live locally? We had no problems with this. Our daughter spent many happy weekends with her friends in London. As it turned out, this was more fun for her than we ever imagined, as the young teens weren't completely supervised by an adult for the entire weekend – something we didn't discover until some years after! Sometimes it's easier not knowing this teenager stuff.

Social, Health and Wellbeing
- Who is the first point of contact at school, to talk about your child's progress/wellbeing, etc.?
- What happens if a child is sick? What access do they have to nursing staff? Under what circumstances will the nursing staff / housemistress contact parents?
- How is boarding accommodation run (e.g. how many pupils to a room, how often are rooms cleaned, etc.)?
- What rules does the school have regarding use of Internet, social media, alcohol, drugs, smoking, etc.?
- How are pupils disciplined for breaking rules? (You need to agree with the stance the school takes on these issues).
- What is the school's policy for telephone calls home / are they allowed access to a mobile phone?
- What are the rules for pupils at the weekend? (e.g. What are/aren't they allowed to do)?
- How much pocket money is recommended per term?

- Are trunks and tuck boxes essential/preferable or unnecessary? How can the school assist with trunks and many suitcases at the end of term? Many schools can't store all the items and require them to be taken from school at the end of each term. Which isn't practical when one child is travelling by air. Thankfully, a company called School Trunk[31] can help you with that!

- What type of food does the school provide at school? Most schools provide a variety to cater for different tastes, including vegan or vegetarian and as an aside, they may also have a tuck shop that sells sweets, snacks, stationery, toiletries, etc.

Sports and Extra-Curricular Activities

- Which sports does the school play competitively? And for fun?

- How many hours a week do pupils play sport?

- Can parents watch matches?

- How far in advance are schools able to list dates for sports events, to facilitate booking of flights?

- What other extra-curricular activities does the school provide (e.g. supervised visits to the theatre, cinema, outdoor adventures, etc.)

- Does the school organise community or fundraising events, and are pupils encouraged to help organise/take part? Not only are such events fun, they build character and help children see the need to be involved in wider social issues at large.

This list is not an exhaustive one, but it may give ideas for further questions of your own. You may even find the answers to some of them on the school website before you visit.

What it will do, is give you an idea of what to look for when you're visiting a boarding school for the first time. You'll soon find that once you've visited more than one, you'll have an instinctive feel for what's right and what's not, as you'll know exactly what you're looking for in terms of its suitability for your child.

As you will only be visiting carefully shortlisted schools, I also suggest you ask your child what they felt about the visit. What they observed overall about the head, teachers, pupils, school's facilities and a general feel for the place. If they can imagine themselves fitting in, that's a good sign you're onto a winner.

I recommend visiting the schools you're considering on your own at first. Then make a *very* short shortlist of your preferred options to take your child to. As you can see, the two-year preparation time wasn't an exaggeration!

UNIVERSITY

A university is an institution of higher (or tertiary) education and research which awards academic degrees in various academic disciplines.
Wikipedia

The chances are, your teen's or young adult's experience of expat life will have nurtured in them a desire to continue travelling.

Nowadays, students don't often take a gap year before or after university. They can just as easily travel while studying abroad. Of course, they may decide to study back home while you're still abroad.

A Pivotal Milestone in a Young Adult's Life

If they do decide to study abroad, they'll be joining the rising number of students who are choosing to do the same. In early 2015, a survey of 2,856 full-time UK students found that 34% said they were considering studying abroad, compared to 20% the previous year.[32] The study showed their reasons varied from, wanting to experience a different culture, to pursuing a unique experience, to building their resume for career-related factors.

Whatever your teen's reason for doing so, it can be an enriching experience, one that will provide them with an impressive set of skills.

I particularly like this comment by J. Mestenhauser of the University of Minnesota, in a research paper titled, "Internationalisation of higher education: a cognitive response to the challenges of the twenty first century" [33]

"When students leave their own cultural environment – for study abroad or academic programmes based on intercultural communication techniques with contents that highlight the international and global dimension of human and social interaction – they have the possibility, for instance, to develop a capacity for adaptation, flexibility, autonomy, to broaden their cultural and intellectual horizons, to increase their levels of intercultural tolerance and interpersonal communication through experiencing different idiosyncrasies."

As always, research is key. As an adult now, your teenager should obviously be encouraged to deal with this themselves, but here is some information so you can support them in this.

What to Study May Determine Where to Study
Your teen may already know what they want to study or have an idea where they want to study. A good starting point is the QS World University Ranking, which can be categorised by either subject, country or university ranking.[34]

If they haven't decided what to study, do encourage them to keep an open mind. Some of the top-ranking universities offer an impressive breadth of subjects that may pique their interest in something they hadn't originally considered.

Visit Open Days

Much of the research will be initially be carried out online, but there's no substitute for visiting the campus itself. A visit will help your teen decide whether they'd enjoy university life in and around the city, or in the quieter suburbs.

A visit will also help them decide what they think about the campus itself, the other students, lecturers, departments and facilities. They'll naturally have an opportunity to visit the departments where they will be studying and even sit in on some of the lectures. This will give them a feel for lecturer's teaching style and an opportunity to ask key questions about the subject and study requirements.

You'll both need to visit the city with a view to finding accommodation – either on campus or nearby. What's the neighbourhood like, is it safe? How reliable is public transport? If they're not living on campus, how far will they need to travel to and from university?

What about student life off campus – shopping, sports centres, nearby clubs and yes, the local nightlife. (Sorry to break it to you, but your little child is growing up!)

As with all educational facilities, you simply can't rely on the pages of a glossy brochure to help you with these questions – you'll both need to visit to get a feel for the place.

I need to reiterate, it's not *all* about the academics, even now!

Visas

As an expat, you're already familiar with applying for travel and residential or other visas. Similarly, your teen will need a student visa to study abroad.

American, Middle Eastern and Australian students here in the UK will need visas to study abroad, but you will find that the process is straight forward, so long as there is sufficient evidence of a university offer.

Students who are resident here in the UK whose first language is not English, need to provide evidence they can speak and write English to a high standard. There are language lessons and exams available to help students become proficient enough to provide this evidence, after which, the visa process should run smoothly.

If your teen wants to come to the UK to study, they will need to meet certain criteria before a visa is granted. For example, they will need to provide evidence of a university offer, can demonstrate that the course will be funded, and that they can speak, read and write fluent English. Full details are listed on the British Council website.[35]

Currently, UK students do not need a visa to study in EU countries, but this could change because of the UK's decision to leave the European Union – we'll have to wait and see what effect this could have on the visa process. UK students who wish to study in the US need to apply online, after which an interview will be arranged at the US consulate.

Applications vary from country to country, so check with relevant Consulates, Embassies and university websites to ensure you follow the process correctly. If in doubt, get on the phone and ensure you get confirmation in writing.

Costs and Fees

Cost is clearly a factor that you'll need to take into consideration.

Tuition fees in the UK are extremely expensive, so it's little wonder that British students are opting to study abroad for their degrees. Fees in the UK can cost £9,000 (approx. US$ 11,250) for home students, or between £10,000 to £20,000 (US$12,500 – US$25,000) for International students.

Venturing further afield, Australia is considered the most expensive place to study, where university fees for International students can cost AUD $15,000 to AUD $37,000 per year (US $11,503 to $28,375). Combine this with living expenses and you rack up a staggering $35,000.

Compare this to studying in what is considered the least expensive place to study, Germany, where fees start from Eur 4,900 (US$ 5,203), or France where fees are EUR 5,800 per year (US$6,158).[36]

Of course, University fees are just one factor. You'll also need to factor in accommodation expenses (if living off campus) plus food, travel and living expenses. No wonder we're called the bank of mum and dad!

[Figures correct at time of going to print]

Erasmus+ Schemes

Erasmus+ (formerly called Erasmus) is the European Union programme for education, training, youth and sport. It runs for seven years, from 2014 to 2020, and organisations are invited to apply for funding each year to undertake creative and worthwhile activities.

There are Erasmus+ schemes held at universities across Europe, which offer students a chance to spend a year studying abroad in another European country. These are universities partnered with the domestic alma mater, but a wide variety of locations are available.

The Erasmus+ website has full details[37], or check whether the university of your choice offers it.

Student Life Abroad

A rising number of universities teach in English, making courses accessible for international students. This is a bonus if your child's main reason for studying abroad is for the experience, rather than to learn another language. But student life abroad won't (and shouldn't) be all work and no play.

The whole point of studying abroad is to experience what other countries offer in the way of culture and adventure, and there are certainly a wide variety of diverse, exciting places to discover.

Italy is host to some of the world's oldest and most prestigious universities, like Padova, while universities in Germany and the Czech Republic offer a cosmopolitan experience alongside courses taught in English to make them more accessible.

Or Singapore, where your teen could study at the National University of Singapore, often ranked one of the top universities in Asia and where all courses are taught in English. They will be exposed to the melting pot of languages, cultures and cuisine Singapore is famous for, and explore South East Asia too.

Japan, Hong Kong, Australia – they're all popular student locations, synonymous with adventure and fascinating cultures.

Wherever your teen decides to study, you will find the larger universities will have clubs where students can make connections with others from their country of origin, so although they will be away from home, they're sure to meet up with others they have something in common with.

SPECIAL EDUCATIONAL NEEDS

If a child can't learn the way we teach, maybe we should teach the way they learn.
Ignacio Estrada

I've established just how important it is to research prospective schools to prepare your child for what will be a tremendous change in their life.

If your child has special educational needs (SEN, or SEND for Special Educational Needs and Disabilities), you'll know just how much more challenging a change in routine – or even just the prospect of change – can be for them.

SEN/SEND care within the school system varies from country to country and sadly, all too often the quality of care is far from satisfactory.

In some cases, it might be possible to accommodate your child's needs, but it's quite likely this will be on a case-by-case basis. For example, some International schools have a special needs program, but they are not bound by any law to provide specialist support, so you can't assume all International schools will have such a program.

On the other hand, national (government funded) schools are bound by law to provide SEN/SEND support. But provision will clearly depend on factors such as the local economy, whether there are sufficiently trained SEN/SEND staff, or simply the efficiency of the school.

Nikki Moffitt is an Australian expat who currently resides in Germany. Her children have been educated in Hong Kong, South Africa, USA and Germany. She explains how she settled her son, on the Autistic Spectrum, into suitable schools along the way.

"If we had known that our son was on the Autism spectrum before we began our expat journey, there is a huge chance we wouldn't have left our home country.

However, once we were away, we powered on, trying to adapt each situation and location to the best type of education for him where possible. We have gotten better at it over the years, and there is no way of knowing if we would have been better staying put in our home country and pursuing all his educational choices there. We are 'at peace' with the choices we have made.

In Durban, South Africa there were no international schools for our children to attend, so they attended a local private school.

In the US, we sent our children to local public schools because they were considered the best option. Our daughter went onto a charter school where she did a Mandarin immersion program, while our son stayed in

140

the mainstream public system where he could have an IEP (individualised education plan) which assisted him with his learning style differences.

Here in Germany, we decided the only option for our thirteen-year old son with ASD was the International school. Putting him in a local, bi-lingual school (or local private) would have been too difficult a transition for him and the associated issues he has with schooling.

We approached the school and asked if they could take our son and offer him some support, and if so, what the options at the school were. They told us they were the only international school in the city so they 'had to take him'. While others may think that's not ideal, I thought it was great. There are so many stories of kids who are differently wired having issues gaining access to education in International schools because the schools are not set up for, leaving expats in the lurch or having to home-school. I can only guess they do this here because home-schooling is not an option in Germany.

My son and daughter love the IB program at the International school. It is not great for my son, because it encourages personal accountability and student led, centred learning. He does tend to need a lot more structure, however for my daughter it is perfect, she is thriving."

The education abroad is often much more dependent on the child rather than the situation or location. If your child is a 'normal' learner with some level of flexibility, the process is straightforward – space in schools permitting. If not, then the situation becomes much more complex and difficult to navigate.

The suggestion from Nikki's experience is that you may simply need to deal with SEN/SEND support on a case by case basis. In any case, each child is an individual, so their ability to settle in will depend on their emotional and social makeup.

Some countries are obviously better than others in their provision for SEN/SEND, as the following list shows. (Please note that I've listed only *some* of the major countries that are typically represented by expats in my experience. If you'd like information on a country I haven't listed, please visit the European Agency for Special Needs and Inclusive Education and select 'Country Information'. The website link is included in Endnotes[38]).

South Africa

Although the South African constitution requires schools to provide special educational allowances to those who need it, provision is sketchy and depends on the area, with better provisions provided in built up areas and towns, than the suburbs.

In 2015, Human Rights Watch[39] stated that impoverished South African children miss out on the right schooling if they have special educational needs, showing that a class divide is very much present when it comes to special education.

However, it is worth researching the facilities in the area you're moving to. If you are living and working in the countryside, you'll most certainly need to organise transport to ensure your child gets the care and attention they need.

The Middle East

Expats who live in the compounds of Oman and Saudi Arabia (e.g. working in the oil industry) have found that it is extremely difficult to organise SEN/SEND support.

Although improvements have been made of late, a report by the British Council suggests the Middle East has an ongoing problem with caring for children with special needs, partly due to an influx of Syrian refugees.[40]

Dubai and other Emirates of the UAE with more integrated communities have a slightly wider range of options. Schools such as Horizon School in Dubai [41], have a policy of providing the right care for a variety of special educational needs, but be aware that schools in Dubai are hard to get into due to heavy over-subscription.

Hong Kong

Hong Kong has a much higher quality of support for SEN/SEND than other Asian countries, with 60 schools dedicated to providing specialist support.[42]

Children can also be integrated into local schools and obtain help for hearing/visual impairments and physical or learning intellectual disabilities. If there are concerns regarding your child's special needs, the school can with your consent arrange to have your child assessed and receive specialist care if appropriate.

UK

SEN facilities in British schools vary. Where appropriate, children should have their needs catered for in a standard school environment[43]. There are, however, dedicated schools for children with more severe needs, plus colleges for older children to gain independence and have access to appropriate higher education.

The Netherlands

The Netherlands holds the reputation for a very high quality of SEN support. The general aim is to find the right educational fit for every child, whatever their need. Those from the UK will find the system not dissimilar to what they are used to at home, if not better.

Dutch educational policy currently aims to reduce the number of children in special schools[44], but will still refer children with more severe needs to specialist educational facilities where appropriate. This allows the curriculum to be tailored to individual students, clearly requiring more effort on the part of teachers and school boards, but at least you as a parent can feel safe in the knowledge your child is getting the SEN support that's right for them.

After I published this online, I had a very useful comment posted which I share below in full;

Helen Claus at Inclusion4all[45] writes:

"Regarding the provision in The Netherlands for children with special needs. The 'Passend Onderwijs' provision is about finding the right school place for each child (as you say) and this is not the same as an inclusive approach, which can be confusing to families new to The Netherlands.

Although there is some provision for supporting children in mainstream education, this remains very limited and many children have to move into special education. There is just not the expertise (yet) amongst mainstream teachers nor the funds to always buy in this support.

The Dutch educational system is organised into Clusters and special schools are generally specialised Cluster schools.

1. Cluster 1: Blind and visually impaired children;
2. Cluster 2: Deaf, hearing impaired and language disordered children;
3. Cluster 3: Physically disabled, cognitive disabled and chronically sick children;
4. Cluster 4: Children with behavioural disorders, developmental disorders and psychiatric disorders.

There is a layer between mainstream and special education at primary school level called Special Primary School. These schools have more expertise, smaller class sizes and children with a range of different learning disabilities.

Families moving to The Netherlands with children with special needs should be prepared for the local school to refer them to special education.

Having said this, there are pockets of good practice and forward thinking, some schools are beginning to be more inclusive, especially in the younger years. Let's hope this continues to develop!

Regarding International education, the majority of schools are (partly) subsidised by the Ministry of Education and they follow the same structure as Dutch schools as regards special education. There is only one

English language special school in The Netherlands for expats. This is the Lighthouse Special Education School in The Hague."

France

In France, there is no legal provision for children with SEN/SEND to be schooled in separate institutions. Instead, the focus is on supporting their needs within the mainstream education. Where mainstream education may not be entirely appropriate, however, some children may receive one-to-one support or taught in a separate class.

Germany

Germany has provisions for specialist schools as well as SEN/SEND support within its mainstream schools, however, parents report that the system can be complicated to navigate. Parents can request an evaluation with a specialist (or specialists) and an assessment will normally recommend a Sonderschule or Förderschule (special educational centres) where SEN/SEND support can be tailored to the needs of the child as appropriate.

BEST PRACTICE FOR CHOOSING A SCHOOL FOR YOUR CHILD WITH SEN

I've simply listed a small selection of countries to show that there isn't a one-size-fits-all solution to SEN/SEND support for your child. It clearly depends on the country you're moving to, and more importantly, the support *your* child needs, and will require very careful research.

Anecdotal evidence from parents who have been through it all (the good, bad and the ugly) is extremely valuable. So, once again, I highly recommend you chat with other expats so that you can make an informed decision, wherever possible.

Aside from researching SEN/SEND support before you relocate, it's a good idea to adopt the following 'best practice', a sort of template for each school that you approach. You'll soon find that you'll quickly identify what seems right and what doesn't:

- Initiate a discussion with your prospective school as soon as possible.
- If your child has a Statement of Educational Needs or an Individual Learning Plan, present this to the school Head, or other appropriate key individuals, so that they can see what type of support your child currently receives. This will help them determine what type of support they might be able to offer you. If the school is unable to offer any SEN/SEND provision, they may be able to suggest an organisation you can turn to for help.
- Wherever possible, select a properly accredited school with specialist support.
- Meet your child's teacher(s) in person as soon as possible. Get to know them so you have a key contact person to approach if you have any concerns about your child's support, and someone who will help you monitor their progress.

Just to reiterate, simply because a school *says* it accepts children with special educational needs, it does not mean a) they will, and b) they are able to accommodate *your* child's specific needs.

Reach out to the schools as soon as possible. I've known at least one family who discovered almost too late that although a school promised SEN provision, their child's place was withdrawn at the last moment. The family had to cancel their entire relocation a month before moving.

Once you've identified a few options for your child's education find out who to talk to at the school regarding their special educational needs provision. Share detailed information about your child's needs and see how they propose to meet them. Find out how their support is delivered; ask how many SEN staff are available and explore their qualifications and experience. And get an admissions acceptance in writing.

I'm sure I don't have to tell you this but don't settle for second best; keep pushing! The right school will do everything possible to help you with the transition, sending you a welcome pack with pictures of teachers, classrooms, toilets, cloakrooms, playgrounds… everything that will help you to give your child a sense of familiarity.

ADVICE FOR STARTING A NEW SCHOOL

Learn everything you can, anytime you can, from anyone you can; there will always come a time when you will be grateful you did.
Sarah Caldwell

Starting a new school is very daunting. Your child must learn new rules, routines and expectations on top of a demanding curriculum and the first few weeks are hard work.

Can you imagine how scary it could be starting a new school in an unfamiliar country? When you add the extra elements of not knowing anyone, not speaking the local language and not having an instinctive feel for the culture, that's an awful lot for a child to process. I've always been incredibly impressed by expat children who do this time and time again!

Get the Timing Right

You may not have control over when you relocate overseas, but if you do have a choice it's worth considering the timing of your move to make life easier for your children. It's a well-documented fact that moving to a new house is one of the most stressful things we ever undertake, and the same stress applies to a child. The chances are that when you move, you'll time it so that you have a few weeks to settle in and explore before you start your new job. Wherever possible, give your child the same period of grace.

Many people choose to move at the beginning of the long school holiday in order to settle in. Plus, it's usually convenient for the adults. However, this isn't always a good idea. Many, if not most, people go away for the holidays, so you won't meet any fellow expats. Schools won't be open (obviously!) so you and your child won't be able to meet school families. And the long school holidays can be a trial with no respite.

Consider moving towards the *end* of the break. This strategy gives you and your children more time with existing friends and you won't be kicking around looking in vain for people to meet in your new country.

Agree a suitable starting date with the school, even if it doesn't coincide with the start of a term, and let your child settle into their new home before they take on the next challenge.

The first day at a new school can be overwhelming and, when thrown in the deep end, a child can feel a sense of dislocation and abandonment. Help your child make the new start as pain-free as possible with these simple tips:

Visit the School
I know this isn't always possible, and if not, sit down with them and virtually 'travel' with to their new school via Google Earth.

With the use of satellite images, you can 'show' them the street they will live, its proximity to the school, even what the school looks like. Ask your child what they imagine their new teachers, or classmates will be like. The more you're able to help them visualise something positive about the relocation, the better prepared they will be when they arrive.

If you *can* visit the school with your child before they start there, that's great. Most schools are receptive to the idea of 'getting to know you' visits and might even be able to welcome you and your child to attend different parts of the day together, to get a feel for the environment. This will give you a chance to meet the teachers, build relationships and for your child to start making some new friends. Even a couple of hours is good, as then your child won't be completely at sea on their first day. This can take a chunk of anxiety away from that 'first day of school' panic.

Perhaps you could agree some half days, individual sessions or extra-curricular activities where your child can join in, safe in the knowledge that it won't be long before you come back. You may have to push for this, but it's well worthwhile. We managed to get our daughter into a couple of half days at the school in Tokyo shortly after we arrived in November/December (she wasn't due to officially start until January). Even though they were reluctant to accommodate, because the school was busy in the run up to the Christmas holidays, they were able to squeeze her in. She achieved more in two half days than she did in a whole term in her first school in England and it made officially starting there a few weeks later much easier for her.

It's all about building confidence. It also helps your child work out the layout of the school, learn where the toilets are, what the routine is for the day, where coats and bags are stored and so on. These all seem like minor details for an adult but for a child they can be a major worry and a distraction from the core purpose of settling into school life, and ultimately, learning.

While there, check out what the current pupils are wearing and carrying: this is particularly important if the school doesn't have a uniform and even more so with pre-teens and teenagers. Most children don't want to stand out from the crowd, so seeing the unspoken 'dress rules' is important. With older children, fitting in socially will override comfort and common sense, so be prepared for the fact that wearing the 'right' shoes or backpack is vital! You may also meet other parents who can help you find your feet in the area.

Find out what items you need to buy before school starts. Some schools provide all stationery while others require you spend a small fortune and source it all yourself. And finding the latter out *after* school has started is not fun – I speak from bitter experience! We didn't find out until *after* the first day of school in Berlin that we were supposed to provide all the very specific stationery. This made for a frantic charge around an unfamiliar city in the evening to find the correct items and got everyone off to a bad start.

Label everything. *Everything.* Items *will* get lost. Make it easier to find in the lost property box by making sure everything has a label on it.

Ask what will be required on their first day of school. Lugging everything, including a PE kit, will not be fun – your child has enough to contend with on that all important first day. My tip would be to simply take a notebook and freshly filled pencil case if you have no input from the school.

Make the journey to school a few times at 'school run' times so you both know the route to and from school and how long it is likely to take.

On the First Day
- Encourage your child from the start to get their school bag ready the previous evening.
- Do not be late. This can spell social disaster for many children.
- With older children, a parent being seen at the school gate can be a huge 'no'! Encourage independence. Let them get on with it and be there if you're needed.

If your child must start at a new school midway through a term, acknowledge how difficult it can be for them. It will be harder for them to make new friends and fit in with an existing peer-group, let alone catching up academically. Provide as much support as you can. Encourage socialisation however you can.

Timetables and Homework
- Make a copy of the timetable. It's useful to have your own copy in case one gets lost or damaged. It also helps you to know when clean PE kit is required!
- Create a homework area at home with the right ambience and equipment to hand.
- Agree when homework will be done and stick to it. The sooner you start this routine the easier life will be when the teenage years hit.
- Expect the first few weeks/months to be an emotional roller coaster for your child and you. There will be a lot of 'trying out' new friendships as well as a lot of settling in and getting used to a new routine. Life can get quite

emotional. Just 'be there' and try not to intervene too much (unless something very serious is occurring, of course).

Keep Talking

It sounds obvious, but your child needs the opportunity to talk to you about what they're going through. Talking things over allows the mind to unravel difficulties and explore solutions. You may well feel that this is a given – of course you talk to your child – but you'll have a lot on your plate too so it's easier to inadvertently trivialise their concerns.

Having said that, this is about balance. You might be feeling anxious about your child's transition and you might be tempted to ask them about every tiny detail of their day. Don't overdo it. Sometimes over-thinking and over-analysing can create anxieties where there are none. Set aside some time each day for a chat. Perhaps this would be when you sit down together to eat. Whatever works for you and your child, provide that opportunity.

Sometimes it's really difficult to get your child to talk. Accept that, and don't force the issue at all otherwise they'll just clam up further. Try asking them, "How did your day go?" This provides the prompt with an open question rather than, "Did you have a good day?" which just requires a yes or no response. From that point on it's often best to let them take the lead and share as much, or as little, as they want. My daughter tends to open up on car journeys; something to do with my attention being on the road and not openly on her. So, try going for a drive!

In the background, do whatever you can to make home life 'safe' and 'normal'. See if you can source some familiar foods, establish a secure routine and try to keep your personal moving-house stress to a minimum. Every little helps.

Forget Their Grades

There's plenty of time for them to catch up. They've just experienced a massive upheaval in their lives, and most children will find fitting in and finding their feet more important than their studies.

What makes a child gifted and talented may not always be good grades in school, but a different way of looking at the world and learning.
Chuck Grassley

For at least the first term or two, grades are not the goal of going to school – unless it's exam time, in which case you may need to be firmer. The main aim of this process is to settle them into their new lives, and to make some friendships with other children who live locally.

I've found it takes at least one term for a child to settle in, and approximately six months, in reality. Some children may take refuge in their studies, in which case, make sure they have enough down time in order to evaluate their new life. Too much perfectionism and overwork can cause problems.

Language barriers, a different curriculum and the generally unsettling experience will almost certainly mean that their grades will suffer, but don't worry about it yet; it's more important for them to make a smooth transition.

Check Out Extracurricular Activities

Find out what after-school and out of school clubs are available.

The more your child gets to see the same faces, the stronger their bond will become and the more confident your child will feel. Find out what after school clubs are available, and get them involved in things like sport, music and drama to develop new friendships and a confident attitude.

There are Girl Guides and Scouting bodies all over the world, so perhaps look up where your local group is so that your child can get involved in these confidence building clubs. You could also look out for expat meet-ups, where your child can enjoy a break from struggling with language and culture and can just relax with some like-minded children from a similar background.

Also look for some non-school related activities too, such as horse riding, rock climbing, swimming and so on. When the inevitable childhood fall-outs occur, it will stand your child in good stead to have a hobby or activity that doesn't relate to school at all. Many communities have sports clubs nearby and they could be a good opportunity for you to get involved and make new friends too.

Throw a Housewarming Party

It could be a chance for you to make some friends in the local community as well.

Once your child has made a few connections at school and in their social lives, invite everyone round for a housewarming party. It will be a great opportunity for your child to cement their blossoming friendships. It could be a chance for you to make some friends in the local community as well.

Be Aware of Potential Issues

Children of different ages handle this whole transition business very differently. The younger your child, the easier transition is. All they want to do is play and be with you. If your child is older, or a teenager, the change will take longer and be harder for all.

Kindergarten Age

Pre-school children are often the most resilient when it comes to a major life change. As long as a parent is around and present, they're OK. Once they've made a friend and learned to communicate with them (which is a much simpler task when you're under five and have toys, sand and water to play with!) they'll feel much happier and will settle in very quickly.

Primary School Age

Primary school children tend to be the ones whose worries are a little more abstract. You might think they're worried about language, learning and making friends but, they're more likely to be distracted by whether they have the right things in their bag, what happens at break time, how the lunch system works and knowing when they can, or can't, go to the bathroom!

You can make their transition easier by finding out exactly what they need before they start. Take this easy-to-solve anxiety away from them. Sort out practical matters like books, pens, pencils, and uniform as far ahead as possible.

Your child may also worry about random 'what if' scenarios: what if my bus doesn't turn up? What if I don't like the food at lunchtime? What if I need to go to the bathroom during a lesson? What if I break my pencil lead? Be steered by your child and prepare them with phrases and solutions to help them.

This also applies to all ages, but your older or younger child may not voice them directly. It's anxiety-based and you can help, whatever their age, by running through the scenarios as if they're a training session. Rather like a fire drill – a "what to do in case of emergency a, b or c" drill.

And on that subject, it will be worth your while asking the school what kind of drills they regularly run. When I was at school, many decades ago, it was just fire drills. However, in Japan, the schools also had earthquake drills which was a little scary initially for my daughter as she wasn't expecting it. However, her training came in extremely useful when we were caught up in the massive magnitude 9 earthquake in 2011 – she made us all get under the table, including the dog.

Even more scary was the 'lockdown drill' they ran in the schools in Germany, and I suspect in most other countries these days. If you're not familiar with these, it's a drill on what to do if an armed intruder comes into the school. Terrifying thought. But you must not hide from the scary things in life, just be prepared.

Make sure they have smart, up-to-date belongings that they can take pride in. You may feel this is an unwelcome expense, but it will help your child feel a lot less anxious. Communication and socialising come easily to most younger children and they'll make connections quickly if they don't have 'trivial' things to worry about.

High School Age

At secondary school age, things get a bit more problematic. From the age of about eleven or twelve children develop a much stronger sense of self-awareness and this is where fitting in becomes more challenging.

At this age, you need to be a lot more guided by your child and undertake a *lot* more planning and preparation. For example, if they'll be attending a local school, giving them the opportunity to learn the language and culture in advance will be helpful.

Find out if the school provides a good settling in process for newcomers and take advantage of it while at the same time remaining on hand yet out of sight... It's a tricky time!

It's extremely unlikely your teenager will choose to share as much with you as a younger child might, so the best way to ensure you're providing the right support is to be there as much as possible and to be observant.

Changes in behaviour, eating habits, mood and appearance can all indicate that your teen is experiencing difficulties, so keep your eyes and ears open. At this age, if problems aren't addressed, they can lead very quickly to mental health issues or anti-social behaviour, so don't be afraid to intervene if you think something is causing a concern.

Keep in Touch With Past Friends

At all ages, your child will feel reassured if they can keep in touch with friends from home or their previous country/school. Most importantly, this lets them know that goodbyes are not forever.

If you're leaving one host country for another and know you won't return, help your children plan how they will communicate with their friends they are leaving behind. One of the things I hear the most from expat children, especially if they don't return to countries they leave, is that goodbye's feel like funerals – many literally go into mourning with every move.

Sending and receiving letters can be a big comfort. Social media really does come into its own here too but keep an eye on what they're doing online. And don't underestimate the value of having the chance to brag a little bit about their new experiences! Feeling that they're having an adventure while things at home are 'just normal', can lend a unique and exciting edge to their transition and can help them to see it in a positive light.

There's no right or wrong answer to settling in; be guided by the needs of your child, keep an open mind and perhaps most importantly, be positive. Don't let your worries – and there are *so* many worries – become their worries.

The good news is the benefits to your child are enormous and children are often better at coping than we give them credit for. But they still need our help and support while they adjust to their new normal.

LEARNING THE HOST LANGUAGE

With languages, you are at home anywhere.
Edward De Waal

Many overseas relocations involve learning a different language. If you're moving to a country where language isn't an issue, you may want to skip this chapter!

If your school foreign language lessons were anything like mine, you were probably sat at your desk with the rest of the classroom, memorising uninspiring rules of grammar *("a noun's gender affects its definite article" – yawn!)*, with a bunch of random phrases *("der Hund ist braun...the dog is brown" versus "Ich sehe den Hund...I see the dog")* and no real idea how to use them. No fun, no passion and not surprisingly, very little stuck.

Speak to any polyglot or language expert and they'll tell you the best way to learn a new language is to completely immerse yourself in it. Yes, learn the basics, but simultaneously get out there and communicate. After all, it is what language is for – to communicate with others. It's fluid, it's social and it should be fun.

How Children Learn a Language

The good news is, children are adept at learning language and a study by William O'Grady, Professor of Linguistics at Hawaii University, gives some interesting clues to why, in his article, *How children learn a language – what every parent should know*.[46]

They Listen

It starts early, where speech can be heard in the mother's womb. The unborn child isn't necessarily able to identify specific words, but they are certainly able to identify patterns and rhythms of speech, or the nuances of the speaker's voice.

In one experiment, mothers-to-be read aloud a story every day during the last six weeks of pregnancy. Some read "The Cat in the Hat" and others read "The King, the Mice and the Cheese". Two days after birth, the infants were tested to see whether they found the story that they'd heard in the womb more soothing than the other story.

Those who heard "The Cat in the Hat" preferred it to "The King, the Mice and the Cheese" and vice versa – even when someone other than their mother read it to them, showing that they recognised the rhythm of the story after birth.

They Recognise Words by Listening and Memorise Chunks of Speech

Children don't sit themselves down with a phrase book to learn words. They simply recognise them by listening and copying. Some are better at recognising words than others and will clearly articulate "mummy", "daddy", etc.

Where other children are particularly good at pronouncing words, they do so by memorising chunks of speech. Their sentences might be poorly articulated, for example *"whassat"*, *"dunno"*, *"donwanna"*, *"gimmedat"*, *"awgone"*, but they're mimicking what they've heard, even if they don't completely understand all the components of the phrase.

They Initially Associate Words With Objects

Children initially associate words with things, so, for example, when you point to a sheep, and say "sheep", that's what it is. In other words, they don't identify the colour of the sheep or the texture of its wool until they're much older. Another association strategy children use is to realise adults usually look at the object they're referring to.

They Make Mistakes (and Don't Worry About Them!)

Who, as a parent, hasn't corrected their child when they've said "went-ed", or "eat-ed"? Once again, they're mimicking what they've heard. They've picked up that when something happened in the past, you add 'ed' to it. That's exactly how past-tense verbs work (in English, at least). They're learning grammatical rules, naturally, by those mistakes.

They Associate Language With an Experience

As O'Grady says, no child has learned to speak by listening to the radio. They learn a language by associating it with what they have experienced, or are about to experience, what they're curious about or what they care about. It's how they figure out what words mean and where to slot them into a sentence.

And here's a fact that amazes me, by the time your child is six years old, they will have a vocabulary of 14,000 words and they will continue learning up to twenty new words every day.

So, far from fearing your child won't learn the host language, you have a little sponge on your hands. If you expose them to the language and culture in the right way, chances are they'll soak it up in no time.

You can even pick up some tips from O'Grady's study for adults trying to learn a language:

- **Listen:** It's a key component to learning a language – to hear the rhythms, patterns, inflections, accents and so forth.

- **Memorise** phrases and chunks of speech: It's far more useful to memorise frequently-used words and phrases, such as "Hi, how are you?" plus typical responses, "I'm fine thanks".

- **Associate the language with things you are interested in**: This is where learning the language can and should be fun. Write down words and phrases that interest you. You could start with "Hi, my name is _____, what's yours?" "I'm from _____ where are you from?" and take it from there. Create your own personal phrase book, rather than use the generic phrase books you find in book shops.

- **Don't be afraid to make mistakes**: This is often where as adults, we fall short. We're good at memorising words, but we're afraid to use them in speech because we're worried we'll make a mistake and will look silly. The fact is, your hosts will be delighted you're trying to speak their language and will be very willing to help. Yes, you may get the occasional giggle when you use the wrong word, (or the right word in the wrong context) but why not laugh it off and simply carry on. The only way to succeed with learning a language is to completely immerse yourself in it – and the only way to do that, is to start speaking it.

START BEFORE YOU MOVE ABROAD

Almost everyone I meet says it's important to start learning the language before you move, and I certainly wish I had made more of an effort.

Frankly, I simply didn't have time to learn Japanese before I moved to Japan. I was busy working, winding-up and then selling my business, packing and dealing with a five-year-old who had just started school. I did, however, download some Japanese courses (Audible[47] have some excellent ones) to listen to on the flight over. Yeah, that didn't go as planned as for once, I slept the sleep of the exhausted on the plane. Also, I watched a fascinating programme in Japanese a couple of days before we flew out, of which I understood precisely nothing. What the programme did do, however, was to give me a sense of the sound and rhythm of the language.

On arrival, and for the first couple of weeks, I didn't understand a word. Not even a single syllable. I couldn't pick out any particular sound whatsoever. Japanese has fewer sound combinations than most languages, so the challenge for English speakers is that words can sound phonetically indistinct. Admittedly, I'm no linguist and find languages a struggle. However, only a couple of weeks after our arrival in Japan, I started to pick out familiar sounds. Syllables and rhythms became distinct and it turns out that the spoken Japanese language isn't as difficult to learn as I expected. Reading and writing, however, is somewhat more complicated.

Something else that worked for me was to have a local radio station on in the car as I did the school runs. Just hearing the sounds, having them around me all the time, meant I absorbed the language subconsciously.

Our daughter took regular lessons at school from the age of five and soon began chattering away in what sounded – at least to me – like perfect Japanese. I have no idea if she was saying real words, but the sounds were absolutely spot on.

Try out an evening class or a home-study course, preferably one that includes videos you can hit pause and rewind to practice. Even if you can't learn to speak well, you will at the very least get your ear attuned, so that when you arrive, the language doesn't sound entirely like gobbledygook!

Take Language Classes in Your Host Country

Once you've relocated and are settled, make it a priority to take language classes. You'll find information of local classes from embassies, fellow expats in your area or failing that the internet. Classes are also one of the best ways to meet fellow expats and potential friends.

If you don't like classroom environments, or find them a bit daunting, I'm sure you could find a one-on-one teacher.

Find an Intercambio or Language Exchange Club

An Intercambio[48], or language exchange club, is a local meet up of people who practice speaking each other's language. Alternatively, if you can't find a local group, why not set up one yourself? Find someone who wants to learn your language (easy if you're a native English speaker as most people want to improve their English) and then organise a time to meet each week. It's a wonderful way to meet native speakers and learn the real language.

Keep It Simple

Start with the basics. Don't be tempted to rush out and buy a conversational Spanish CD and force your child to listen and repeat. Instead, try to remember the fun you had together when they first learned to talk. Invest in (or even make) some bright and fun flashcards that label everyday people and objects – mum, dad, brother, sister, dog, cat, table, chair etc.

Use them little and often. One your child is familiar with them, make a game out of it by placing the cards face down and seeing whether they can remember the correct word. You'll be amazed at how quickly they learn the basics, if you remember to make it fun.

Something else that worked well for us, was to choose a DVD of one of our daughter's favourite programs (I seem to remember 'Charlie and Lola' was a recurring theme). At the start of the program, we'd choose the language we could play it in. While we were in Japan, we obviously chose Japanese, and while in Germany we watched it in German. We watched those programs so often, even I can remember some of the vocabulary, having had it engrained in my subconscious.

Learning Takes Time

Once you feel confident your child has a varied range of words and can name most familiar household objects, start to learn phrases and conversation together.

But try to avoid labelling the learning – remember those awful French lessons at school when you had to learn different tenses, verbs, adverbs and so on? Focus instead on reading simple books together and using the pictures as prompts to understand what's going on or watching a familiar film together and changing the language settings.

Focus on everyday words phrases and say them to each other as often as possible – *"I love you"; "please pass me that book/plate/cup"; "it's raining/sunny/windy today"; "shall we go to the park?"* Using common household phrases and making a game out of only saying them in the host language will encourage frequent use and fun learning.

And count everything. Numbers are rhythmic, so they're easily remembered and of course, always useful.

Learn Together

Young children love to teach. Remember the 'pretend schools' you may have played when your children were little? A fun way to learn a new language, especially if your child is having formal lessons, is to have them teach you what they have learned.

As well as having fun, there is another key element to learning the language – patience. Don't rush to try to teach your child to converse in a day. It will take months, so start early. Think back to when they first learned to talk, this is no different. There will be times when they will feel frustrated and won't feel like complying – don't push them. If they can relax and enjoy the learning process in the knowledge that you won't be cross if they're tired or get it wrong, they will learn quickly and easily.

As time goes on, build on your progress more and have a time during the day – for example around the dinner table – when the conversation is solely in the language being learned. Or if you have a family friend who is fluent already, have the person talk only the host language. Don't worry if not everything is understood. If you've worked through the basics, you will all understand enough to follow the gist and the rest will flow naturally.

Ultimately, learning the language will increase opportunities for you and your child. You don't need to become a master, but you do need to be able to communicate. Focus on what's going to be useful for your time there, as opposed to pages of unrelated vocabulary.

Let's face it, not learning the local language will make every day experiences stressful – such as going to the doctors, shopping, getting your car serviced, and so forth. Often, it's the simple things you take for granted, that become a minefield when you're in an unfamiliar land.

~~~~~

WHY WE CHOSE FULL IMMERSION

ExpatChild Survey: Mary Johnson, Switzerland

We opted for full immersion because we wanted our kids to learn the language, make new friends nearby, and be integrated into our new community. We live in a nice area in the middle of a Swiss village – why would we not want them to mix?

We were also on a limited time with the firm paying for international schooling and there wasn't the option of bilingual schooling at that point (not that we would have been able to afford it), so full immersion at the local school seemed the best option.

They were very tired because of the language immersion, but they quickly made friends. The biggest shocks were the cultural factors e.g. coming home for lunch, kids being sent home from school if a teacher was sick (rather than the school finding a cover teacher) or differing timetables with little shared block time etc. – but perhaps that was more me than them.

Having to learn how to write all over again (the Swiss way) was a bit of a pain, as my elder son was in Grade 4, but he coped. My son is left-handed. His teacher found him a left-handed fountain pen and the handwriting exercise book was a left handed one too, so they tried their best to accommodate him.

With the benefit of hindsight, is there anything you'd do differently?

My younger son had a rough start at school with a useless teacher in Grade 2-3 and a bullying teacher in Grade 4-6. I might have fought more with the teacher, but it wasn't worth my son being ostracised because of us being difficult parents.

It worked out in the end because his teacher at Secondary school was outstanding, and he wouldn't have been in that class had it not been for the bully teacher in Grade 4-6 (long story).

Even though the kids are no longer in touch with their friends from the International School (most of whom have moved on from Switzerland), I still have a number of friends who were both mothers and teaching staff and part of my initial friendship group.

It's been a rough ride at times, but my kids are now Swiss, with dual citizenship and feel that they belong. We've not regretted it for a moment.

What tips would you give parents considering full immersion?

Don't underestimate how exhausting it is for the child. Full on language immersion is a killer. Don't make them do lots of extra activities because you think they are falling behind with their mother tongue. They are absorbing a whole new language, and they will catch up. You need to give them time and space. Don't crowd them.

Give them the emotional and domestic structure to cope but allow them the time and space to breathe and absorb what they are learning. It's much harder on them than it is for you – even if it is frustrating that you can't understand letters sent home from the school!

Our elder son's teacher (who was lovely and completely on our side), refused to speak English with us for the whole of our first parent's evening, just to show us what our son was having to cope with each day. We appreciated that, because it made us really stop and think about what our kids were going through.

RAISING A BILINGUAL CHILD

*One language sets you in a corridor for life. Two languages open
every door along the way.*
Frank Smith

Here's a common myth about raising a bilingual child, "That
child at playgroup can't talk properly because his parents
insists on teaching him two languages; it's confusing for the
poor little soul." A myth, and wrong... here's why.

It's widely understood that the unborn child can differentiate
between different linguistic patterns and that after birth, they
can quickly recognise the vocabulary in each one. There's
every chance that the earlier you teach your child multiple
languages, the easier it will be for them to learn.

The Perceived Risks

Now, almost all myths have some underlying truths so let's
get this out of the way from the start.

Yes, there is some evidence that a baby exposed to multiple
languages may start to talk slightly later than a baby exposed

to only one. However extensive research has proven that once talking, their developmental patterns and speed show no significant variance; in fact, they learn much more about decoding languages and will find it easier later in life to progress this skill and learn others too.

It is also true that toddlers taught two or more languages sometimes muddle their speech – but don't all toddlers? And they may at times even interchange words and phrases from the languages they're exposed to in the same conversation.

There's a simple reason for this, and it's not as alarming as some people think. From birth until three, a child is still in the process of mapping out linguistic patterns. Depending on what exposure they've had to each of the languages being taught, their vocabulary may vary from one language to another. So, it is perfectly logical for them to use the word they *know* as a substitute in a sentence for the word they're not yet familiar with.

"Want to play *bola*!" is a simple example. This child is learning English and Spanish, so they know they want to play ball and can express the desire, which is fantastic. They can't remember the English word for ball, so simply substitute a Spanish word.

No big deal. Respond in English "Yes, let's play *ball*" and maybe they will remember it next time.

Structure and Exposure

The best way to raise a bilingual child is to talk a lot and worry very little.

Get the whole family involved, be committed to your goal and be flexible but have a structure. Structure is important.

For the child to become fluent in both languages, there needs to be enough exposure to each and sufficient time to practise.

Let's take an example, a common scenario. A child is being taught both Spanish (native) and French. In this scenario, the family lives in Spain, which is their Father's home country. The Mother is French. She wants the child to speak her native tongue to communicate with Grandparents etc., so the decision has been made before the child is even born, to teach both languages.

There are two basic structures that most people use; adapted slightly to meet their own requirements.

One Parent One Language (OPOL)

The first and perhaps the most effective structure, is One Parent One Language (OPOL). This means that each parent will communicate with the child only in his or her native tongue.

This is an excellent way to ensure there is exposure to both languages, but there are some things you need to consider. As the child gets older, they'll attend school, where the language will be local. In the case of our example family, this means the child's majority language will be Spanish. To learn fluent French (the minority language) studies suggest they would need to hear and speak it up to 30% of their waking time.

In other words, the parent speaking the minority language will need to spend enough time talking to and playing with the child – which might not work, if mum is teaching the minority language and she doesn't get in from work until seven o'clock every night, just in time for bath and bed.

What could potentially happen, is that the child will learn enough vocabulary to communicate with mum during those times but will not feel it necessary to widen the vocabulary and become fluent in conversing with others.

Minority Language at Home

This method means that in the home, everyone speaks the minority language (in the case of our example family, French) and the child is exposed to the native or majority language at playgroups, nursery, school etc.

This method can work well for expat families preserving the language of their home country, but will not work for our example family, unless dad also speaks fluent French.

One potential disadvantage to this method, is that from birth, the child will learn only the minority language and will not begin learning the other (the majority, which in our example family's case is Spanish) until they mix with other children and adults.

However, the child will soon catch up if they attend playgroups or nurseries from an early age and are fully immersed in the native language outside the home.

Tips to Help Your Bilingual Child With Language

You can teach a child a second language at any age although due to the speed of their cognitive development under seven years-old is the optimal time for them to find it relatively easy.

Other people delight in having opinions about the way your children are raised and you will inevitably hear lots of negativity about confusing the poor mite. Ignore them. You are giving your child an enormous cognitive advantage!

Do your research. Being fluently bilingual doesn't happen by accident and you need to ensure that you are structured enough to enable the child to get the most out of the learning experience. There are excellent resources to help you, you just need to search for what inspires you and your child.

A child learns through play. Don't try to formalise learning; make it natural. Buy board games, books, maps, puzzles, DVDs, computer apps etc. in the minority language and watch as your child learns without even realising it. You'll find excellent resources in different languages on Amazon, suitable for a variety of different age groups.

Don't forget that speaking a language fluently doesn't go hand in hand with being able to read and write in that minority language. Use flashcards, comic books, story time and game. Stick funny labels, posters and poems around the house to make learning and reading fun.

Songs – even in the background – are a fabulous teaching tool. Have songs in the minority language playing quietly at home and in the car; you'll be amazed at how quickly your child will be singing along.

Above all, you're doing this to give your child the best possible start as a bilingual person.

KEEPING UP WITH ENGLISH IN A FOREIGN COUNTRY

Language is the road map of a culture. It tells you where its people come from and where they are going.
Rita Mae Brown

A common challenge when bringing up young English-speaking children in a foreign country, is when and how to introduce written English.

It's one thing to expect a child to learn how to speak two languages at the same time, but is it an unnecessary pressure to expect them to cope with learning the different written spellings and pronunciations of two languages at the same time?

Nikky McArthur, who writes a blog 'A Mother in France' gives her experience of raising her children in France and helping them retain their written and spoken English.[49]

How We Helped Our Children Retain Their English in France.

My biggest concern was that my children would not be able to read and write in English. I've heard of cases of English-speaking teenagers with very poor written skills. What a wasted opportunity to be orally bilingual, but not able to read and write in both languages too. It obviously won't just happen automatically without at least a little gentle encouragement, but when is the right time to start introducing it?

Our second eldest was ten when we moved to France, so he was already competent in reading and writing in English. We never had to do anything special with him to keep up his English, other than encourage him to read and keep in touch with English friends and family (mainly through Facebook and MSN). He's eighteen now and studying at University in Montpellier. He is fully fluent in French, but he prefers talking, reading and writing in English.

Our three youngest children are different. They have only attended French schools and are learning to read and write in French first. French is very different to English and I think it's a lot to ask a five or six-year-old (or younger) to try and learn both methods of reading and writing at the same time. I didn't want to make the learning process more difficult for them at school. We had no intention of returning to the UK, so didn't feel there was any rush with their English.

French Mastery First

We decided to take a more organic approach. We didn't do any formal teaching of reading or writing in English until they'd mastered the basics of French. We spoke exclusively in English at home, we read to them in English and they are exposed to English on TV, but we didn't sit down with them and try to teach them to read and write in English while they were starting to learn to read and write in French.

James was about seven nearly eight when he started showing an interest in learning to read English. I let him take the lead, as if I had tried to force him, he would only have resented it. He was playing games on the computer which often have instructions in English. He was tired of having to ask me what they said – he wanted to be able to read himself and he asked if we could teach him.

I bought him some English early readers, not complete beginners, but books appropriate for his age or maybe slightly younger to start with. I sat with him for a short time most evenings while he attempted to read them. At first, he would naturally read them as he would French, processing the letters on the page to form words from his knowledge of French sounds. I would gently correct him and within a few weeks he was correcting himself. He could already speak English fluently, so he knew when the words he was producing sounded incorrect.

Motivation to Learn

It really helps if the child is exposed to things that will motivate them to learn. No one enjoys learning if they can't see an advantage to it. Make sure that the benefits of reading and writing are clear and 'because it will be useful to you in later life' is not an incentive for a child of any age.

I'd say from my experience, don't push English too soon, but don't leave it too late either. Let your child take the lead where possible. Wait until they've mastered the basics of their adopted language. When they begin taking an interest in learning to read English, start to gently introduce English books first, then gradually encourage them to start writing. Write to their friends and family, birthday and Christmas cards, letters to Santa, thank you notes, postcards etc. Then once they're starting to get more confident, you can encourage them to use their English in a more creative way – write a story or a poem etc. If you prefer you can see if there are some local classes for English children in your area or opt for an on-line course. There are many resources out there.

Whether you choose to introduce English simultaneously with learning French or wait till later, the most important thing is that you help to create an atmosphere where your children can enjoy developing a language that comes easily to them. If they are motivated to learn, then you won't have to force them to do it. Keep it light and fun and if they're resisting don't push it, wait a few months before you try again. Avoid transferring your concerns and anxieties onto them or you'll be making it more difficult in the long run.

Trust that given the right encouragement, your child will learn in their own time. Children have an inbuilt curiosity and capacity to learn and they'll tell you when they're ready, you just have to be receptive to the signs.

HOW TO HELP YOUR CHILD RETAIN THEIR SECOND (OR THIRD) LANGUAGE

Lynn Schreiber, a British writer who has lived and worked in Germany and Switzerland, spent four years in Geneva with her husband and their children attending a French-speaking school.

Lynn explains how she and her husband helped their children retain their French and German after returning to the UK.[50]

How We Helped Our Children Retain Their German and French

After four years in a French-speaking school, we were keen for our children to retain both German and French when we returned to UK. I wasn't worried about their German language skills, as my husband is German, and we speak German at home, but how to manage their third language, French, which neither of us spoke fluently?

These are some of the things we found helpful:

Listen to Online Radio

There are countless apps for smartphones which enable the user to listen to radio stations from around the world. Perhaps you had a favourite station when you lived abroad – choose one that broadcasts a mix of chatter and music. This also gives kids some continuity and helps them keep up with news from the place you've just left.

Meet Native Speakers

The ease of finding other speakers of the language obviously depends where you live, and how unusual the language is. If you're moving from Paris to London, then you'll have no trouble finding other French speakers. You may not want to start formal classes, and from my experience it can be quite tricky to find classes of the appropriate level for more fluent children. If you can find a group of people who speak the language, preferably with children, and meet up occasionally, then this can help keep the language alive.

Private Classes or Tutoring

As mentioned, it can be difficult to locate a class that teaches at the appropriate level for your kids. Group lessons for kids are too easy for them – they'd be bored with learning the colours and singing nursery rhymes. Adult classes are too advanced, both in the topics discussed and the attention to grammar. A private tutor is often more appropriate, but it is important to keep these lessons fun and engaging. The 'lessons' can be spent playing board games, baking, doing crafts, or even doing their regular homework, but in the second language.

Trips Abroad

This is a tricky one, because you might not want to go back to the place you've just left all too soon. For kids who are really missing their friends, it can be like tearing off a sticking plaster, just as the wound was almost healed. Leaving again could set them back in their acceptance of your new home. Choose another country, where the language is spoken, but doesn't hold such precious memories, and won't be such a wrench to leave again.

Use Social Media

The advent of social media networks means that it is much easier for young people to keep in touch with their friends when they move away. Instagram is incredibly popular with tweens and teens and is an effective way for them to exchange short messages, or even videos with their friends. Video calling, using Skype, Google Hangouts or FaceTime, helps to keep the language skills fresh and up-to-date.

Be Flexible

Research suggests that even if a person has no active memory of a language, there is a residue left in the brain, for a very long time.[51]

Your child won't forget their second language immediately, so let them take some time to come to terms with the move first, if they are reluctant to engage.

Language skills are peculiar and seem 'hide' somewhere in the brain for many years. As one of the many Brits who struggled to learn French at school during the 1970s, I never used it once after I left school. Over three decades later I was fortunate to holiday in Mauritius and, suddenly, much of that schoolgirl French came back to me!

If the school you're considering doesn't offer the languages you'd like your child to learn, or if you're concerned about your child missing out on the opportunity to learn the language or languages of the country you have moved to, then organise after school activities or a language partner for your child with local children. This makes the language learning more enjoyable and less institutionalised. It is also an opportunity to make friends outside of school and learn more practical aspects of the language, such as colloquialisms.

Alternatively, consider finding a private tutor to teach the language. We found a fabulous Japanese language tutor when we lived in Berlin. She came to our house every week and enabled our daughter to keep her Japanese language skills sharp.

It is important to encourage your child's learning with this. You may even want to take some conversation classes yourself so that you can practice with your children.

My teenage daughter has a novel way of refreshing her language skills; she sets her mobile phone to the language she wants to work on so is seeing it all the time.

So, encourage your child to keep up with the languages they have learned during your expat life, but don't force it on them. As I'm sure we're all aware, the more you force a child – especially a teenager – to do something, the less they are willing to do it.

COPING WITH REPATRIATION

Home is a name, a word, it is a strong one; stronger than magician ever spoke, or spirit ever answered to, in the strongest conjuration.
Charles Dickens

When you spend every few years packing, unpacking, settling in, moving on and repeating the cycle all over again, coming home feels like a strange mixture of excitement and uncertainty.

Excitement because it's always nice to see old friends and familiar faces and places.

Uncertainty, because while you've spread your wings and 'grown' while away, others back home haven't. Your world view has grown exponentially, and it can be hard to relate to people who haven't lived overseas. There's a myriad of experiences you want to share, that non-travellers simply don't or can't understand, and that's something that can be incredibly frustrating.

Turn that around though; your 'people back home' have also grown and changed just as much as you have. Nothing stays static. You've all changed, just in different ways.

Home though, is tricky to define. Look up any dictionary and you'll find among the many definitions:

Home: *Noun* – The place where one lives permanently. (As expats, we don't live in one place permanently).
Adjective – Relating to one's own country. (Still tricky to define if you were born en-route during your parent's travels and brought up more than one country).

For me, it's wherever I am *right now*, among the people I love and want to be with. It must be, otherwise I would always be hankering after something else.

My husband only refers to home as the UK, perhaps because he works with a lot of British people.

Our daughter's response to this question of 'home' however, is more confused. She has a very strong affinity to Japan as that is where she spent her most formative years from the age of five until ten. She knows she is British, but having spent twelve years overseas, there is much of the British teenage culture she is unaware of; but she's learning quickly!

We moved back to the UK in February 2018 – so we have been back less than a year at the time of this book going to press. And it is the hardest move I have ever made.

Everyone told me it would be, so I was somewhat prepared. But what I wasn't prepared for was just how much my home country has changed in the past twelve years.

I strongly believe that if the home environment – wherever you are at this moment in time – is calm, welcoming and as familiar as possible, your child will cope. When you create a comforting haven for your them, they will settle much more easily. So, I have spent the past few months trying to make this house a welcoming and cosy home. It hasn't been easy, as we battle general day-to-day life, like finding leaks in the house, registering with doctors, finding dentists and so on. At least here, I know the language and the basics of getting around, but the rules and regulations in the UK have changed enough to make it a slight struggle.

Then there's a new kind of education for my daughter, too. Due to her age when we returned – sixteen and a half years old– she couldn't get into any school in this area. This wasn't helped by the government changing the education rules and exams last year, making it more complicated. She left school in South Africa in November 2017 and couldn't start education in the UK until September 2018. So, that's been 'fun'!

She's now attending the local college, but that's only for a couple of days a week. Due to her expat life, she doesn't find it hard to make new friends. And her teachers have noted their surprise at how she communicates well with all adults too – something that teenagers here seem to have difficulty doing. There is very little public transport here and she's very isolated. Thankfully, she has managed to keep in touch with friends made over the years in other parts of the country, so we have helped her get out to see them as much as possible. It's still early days, in repatriation terms, but I feel it's going well.

If you've been away for a relatively short time, a couple of years or so, everyone may expect a seamless transition. But the fact is, your children won't necessarily be able to slide back at school, or among former social groups, as if nothing's happened.

Expectations and assumptions are our downfall. Don't make them!

Naomi Hattaway who founded the community "I am a Triangle – and other tips for repatriation"[52], describes the challenge as feeling you don't fit in, you don't blend in, despite your efforts to integrate.

As I mentioned before, our children have seen far more of the world than their untravelled counterparts have. In many respects, they've matured, blossomed and grown up quicker. They have a world view that their counterparts may not have. This can be difficult for them to handle, but here are some ways you can help your child cope with repatriation:

Recognise That Everyone Changes

Help your children see that although they feel changed by their experiences abroad, *everyone* has changed. Your child's travels are only a part (albeit a major part for them) of what has moulded and shaped them into the person they are. Their friends have changed to, through different experiences back at home. Encourage your child to share their experiences, but also show as much interest in their friend's experiences too.

Make New Friends

Expats are brilliant at adapting to new, foreign cultures. This skill will put your child in good stead when they're back at home. Encourage them to make new friends, particularly new friends that may be visiting from countries you've visited. They will have something in common and will be able to exchange stories they're familiar with.

Stay Connected With the Expat Community

Encourage your child to lean on expat friends if at all possible, particularly those who have also repatriated. They're likely to be the only ones who truly understand what they're going through.

This is easier said than done though. I haven't met anyone in the town where I live who has ever left the area. Therefore, I doubt there are children my daughter's age who are ex-expats.

Seek Emotional Help and Support

Don't dismiss their feelings of grief or loss of former friends and countries. Expats and TCKs can genuinely feel a stranger in their home country, or country of their passport. If things get tough, look for professional help.

Home As a Concept, Not a Tangible Place

As I mentioned earlier, for me, home is here right now with the people I love spending time with. While I'm not encouraging you to negate the feelings your child might be going through, help them realise repatriation *will* get easier over time if they see a homecoming, not necessarily as a place they must fit in to, but a frame of mind they can gradually accept. It will, and should, take time.

Their point of view will have changed. The way they identify with others and things around them will have changed. But that's all OK. They don't *have* to feel settled immediately – in fact, you don't have to try to 'fix' things for them either. It's good for them to just have an outlet to talk and pour out what they're feeling – the frustration, the good, bad and ugly.

Ultimately, who's to say there's anything wrong with being transient?

Count Your Blessings

While I'd hate this to sound trite, if you've travelled to economically poorer parts of the world, you'll understand what I mean by 'count your blessings'. Electricity that doesn't sudden cut out on you; telephones that work all the time; hot and cold running water from a tap; clean hospitals; police that don't need to be bribed. I could go on. While you've probably shielded your child from some of these, there will be many they will have noticed for themselves. We all have a lot to be thankful for. It's good to remind ourselves of what those things are occasionally.

When daily life in another country sharply shows you the big things such as starvation, poverty and murder, the change when you move back to your 'safe' and developed home country where the main topic of conversation is make-up, or eyebrows, or television shows, can be shocking.

It's Not Their Home

When you're my age and you've lived overseas for twelve years, that's only a small fraction of your life. Twelve years, however, is the majority of my teenage daughter's life.

My home country is not *her* home country. She can vaguely remember living here – we left a few weeks after her fifth birthday. Of course, we have visited England over the years, but those trips were only holidays to her; similar to the holidays we took to Bali or Mauritius.

We must not assume that our children will recognise our home as theirs.

IN CONCLUSION

It's not hard to make decisions when you know what your
values are.
Roy Disney

Hopefully the previous chapters have given you a clearer idea
on how to go about choosing the right school for your child.

Work out what your values are, what your child needs and
what works for your entire family. And then be prepared to
change all that if it doesn't work out.

To recap on what you really need to consider:

- Age of your child
- How long are you going to stay in that country?
- Where are you moving next?
- How different is the curriculum going to be?
- Language considerations
- Can you support your child in a new school?
- Special educational needs

- How far away from your home is the school?
- Does the school day fit in with your lifestyle?
- How will the school run work?
- How does the school 'feel'?

If you're moving overseas with the intention of settling permanently, then you may find a local school or, if available, a bilingual school is your best bet. If it's a short-term assignment and you'll be returning to your home country, a British, American, Canadian or International Baccalaureate school might offer your child a way to repatriate more easily. Or, if you're planning to keep moving then an IB school, a group school or a broadly international school might allow your child to embrace his or her nomadic lifestyle.

Which type of school you choose for your child may be governed to some extent by your future plans. And it may be governed by what is available to you in your new home town, and feasible for your life in general. And it must be governed by your child's individuality.

YOUR CHILD, YOUR CHOICE

But the fact is, no matter how good the teacher, how small the class, how focused on quality education the school may be none of this matters if we ignore the individual needs of our students.
Roy Barnes

Remember, that even within the school categories described in this book, individual schools will vary. Look carefully at the culture behind each international school on offer and consider what sort of educational experience you want your child to have. It's all well and good to choose your ideal school type but make sure the individual school can live up to your expectations.

While a local school may suit children who will be in the country for several years, or permanently, truly international schools are the better option for those who move around frequently. If your first language is English, or if your child has ambitions to work internationally, the education in English will ensure that they have a good basis for business, education and socialising. Languages can be picked up at any time.

Full immersion in a different language school is very difficult indeed and should really only be attempted if you're going to live there permanently, or at least for the length of their schooling. And it's best to start them in this system as early as possible. Toddlers attending a host-language kindergarten will cope a bit better than a thirteen-year-old in a school where they speak none of the language.

Naturally, I'm *not* saying don't do this, but do be prepared for the sheer exhaustion and frustration you will all feel, as explained in Mary's interview earlier.

School websites, inspections and grades can only tell you so much; the experiences of children at those schools and the opportunities available to them are a much better measure. You may find that in some places, the local schools are much better than international ones. However, the general consensus on the international school system is that they provide a diverse social experience as well as a comprehensive education. As always, checking before you move is your best option.

By taking an interest in your child's education, you can help support them to integrate and adapt to their new surroundings. It's never easy getting used to a new country and education system, but with the right support children are incredibly adaptable.

Remember, This is a Very Personal Decision

I'll keep saying this; choose a school for *your* child.

And, it is not the end of the world if you happen to choose a school that is not a good fit for your child. Naturally, you wouldn't intentionally choose the wrong school for your child, of course, and you won't know the school isn't a good fit for your child until they've been there a while. You can always change your mind if it's not working out for any reason and you should not be afraid to do so.

Often, you'll know fairly quickly if a school is not likely to work out well for your child, but I would suggest waiting a term to see if your child settles in their new environment. It takes this long for them to work it all out, especially when they're older. However, if there are serious issues, such as bullying, lack of support for gaps in their education or poor SEN provision, it's better to pull them out sooner rather than later. To leave a child in a damaging environment is worse for them in the longer term.

Your child will adapt to expat life quicker if they're happy at school. After all, they spend a good deal of their life at school, so it makes sense to make sure they are at the best one for them.

Choosing a school is a minefield wherever you are in the world. I hear friends from my home country agonising over it too but choosing a school in a different country is a different kind of challenge.

Ultimately, it should be a very personal decision. A decision that as parents we can only hope is for the best.

Too much emphasis is sometimes put on trying to find a 'good' school. What is more important is that your child is happy there.

A happy child learns, regardless of the school's reputation.

EPILOGUE

*Good decisions come from experience, and experience comes
from bad decisions.*

The process of compiling and writing this guide has been
both stimulating and uncomfortable.

Stimulating, because it got me recalling so much of what
worked out well for us in our various challenges in finding a
suitable school. I didn't have anyone to turn to for advice, so
it gives me satisfaction knowing I can pass on this knowledge
to you. If this guide helps you make choosing a school
overseas less stressful, then my work here is done!

Uncomfortable, because it has also meant looking back on
some of the mistakes we made and recalling where things
went horribly wrong. Suffice to say, there is no magic wand,
and equally, nothing is ever written in stone.

Between the ages of five to seventeen years old my daughter
has attended eight schools in four countries, including the
college she is now attending back in the UK.

Unsurprisingly, I wouldn't recommend *quite* so many changes, but in our case, it was better for her to change schools at those points, rather than stay in ones that weren't right for her.

A couple of those schools were 'the ones that all other expat children went to', so proves this isn't always the best option for *your* child. On the flip side of that sentiment, you may be in a country where the expat community is restricted – in size and in cultural norms there – and international schools usually do understand your peripatetic life in a way that the local community does not.

One of the schools we moved from changed from an international school, with all lessons in English, to a local language school over the summer holidays! The admissions officer 'neglected' to tell us this every time we talked to them, even though they knew it would be happening. We discovered this information, by accident – we overheard someone talking about it –on the last day of term. It still makes me cross all these years later.

I've endeavoured to be as honest as I can with my own experiences. It doesn't serve anyone's interest if I gloss over what can possibly go wrong when you're trying to settle your child somewhere new. Yet, in the sense of discretion and privacy, I have left out a lot of information about what we, as a family, and our daughter in particular, has gone through. Suffice to say, we didn't change schools so often simply because we 'felt like it'.

Equally, some of our interviewees have been as candid with their responses too. I think these have been very helpful and if you can relate to what they've been through, perhaps it will help you weigh up the pros and cons of the suitability of the school you're considering for your child.

When I look back at our choice of schools – both good and bad – I'd probably round up by giving the following two final pieces of advice:

DON'T HESITATE TO CHANGE SCHOOLS IF YOUR FIRST CHOICE DOESN'T WORK OUT.

We agonised over whether to change schools on each occasion because we hoped things would work out in the end. They didn't work out and I wish I had been quicker in acting to remove her from certain schools sooner.

DON'T DISMISS A SCHOOL WITHOUT GIVING IT DUE CONSIDERATION.

It's very easy to be swayed by opinion, gossip or hearsay. Simply do your own research, do what is best for *your* child given *your* unique circumstances and go with your gut instinct. I really didn't want our daughter to go to boarding school because sending a child away from home is such an emotive issue. Yet she absolutely loved it and to this day, keeps in touch with the friends she made there.

And another school I had dismissed due to a starting age restriction turned out to be perfect for her. Rather than go by what was on their website, I called the school in desperation to see if there was any leeway, and it transpired they simply hadn't had chance to update their website with the new admission ages.

As expats, we are innovative, adaptable, forward-thinking creatures. We know there's always a Plan B. And if you don't have a Plan B you need to make one quickly! And if Plan B doesn't work out, there's always a Plan C. And, let's be honest, a whole lot of other letters of the alphabet.

I think it's important for you to remember that nothing is set in stone – you *can* make changes. When you're moving abroad with children, nothing beats ensuring their happiness.

All in all, it is my sincerest hope that this guide has provided you with a better understanding of how to choose a school overseas, and that you'll feel able to do so as smoothly as possible.

SO, WHAT'S NEXT?

Well, it could be that you're planning an imminent move abroad. If you are, have you considered just how much goes into planning, organising and shipping your entire life abroad? Perhaps you're in the very early stages of thinking about moving overseas, with no real idea of if it's the right decision for you and your family?

Do you truly know what to expect when you're expatting? This book 'only' covers expat education, but there is so much more to prepare for when moving overseas to live.

DID YOU KNOW THAT ALMOST HALF OF ALL INTERNATIONAL ASSIGNMENTS FAIL?

Most of these failures can be traced back to a lack of realistic preparation. Expat life can be shocking for some people as expectations don't match real life. There are so many small, but significant details to consider that it's easy to get caught by surprise. You will be amazed at how small things can affect your daily life when living in a different culture, miles from everything familiar.

And bad things can, and do, happen in the 'dream expat life', just as they do everywhere.

Being properly prepared helps minimise anxiety and reduces stress and the possibility of decision fatigue and mental paralysis. I have lots of tips and tricks for you.

Talking things through with someone who has been through all this before helps a great deal. I'm here for you; just let me know what you'd like me to support you with. Consider me a combination of Virtual Assistant, Expat Life Mentor and your best friend!

Being treated as an individual is crucial to your well-being. Everyone is different, and every relocation is different. If you follow the crowd, doing 'what all other expats do', you're not setting yourself up for your dream expat life. Often when you get advice, you're hearing what other people think you should do – because it worked for them. This is why it's difficult to sift out the information you need.

I would love to help you with all this.

Why not send me an email – hello@expatability.net – and find out how I can help you with your move abroad?

So, if you're relocating overseas for the first time, or even if you just want to be more organised with your current relocation plans, please do get in touch. I can help *you* navigate the challenges of moving and living abroad with *your* family.

I look forward to chatting with you!

Carole

🌐 https://expatability.net

🌐 https://expatchild.com

✉ hello@expatability.net

PRAISE FOR CAROLE'S WORK

I had been in South Africa with my husband and two children aged eleven and sixteen for two months when I first 'met' Carole online. The children were settled in school and my husband in his job and the honeymoon period had come to an end for me. I'd had given no thought to what I was going to do personally or professionally during the moving process, and to be honest I was regretting the move.

Whilst searching for information online I 'met' Carole. Despite Carole and her family going through the whole relocation again themselves with a young child, they were also dealing with the trauma and upheaval of when the earthquake and tsunami that stuck Japan two days earlier.

Carole took time to advise me of the steps/mountains I would reach, in what order and when and what the next hurdle would be. She warned me of the pitfalls and gave me advice on how to handle things and really helped me to understand the process of life as an expat. *Suzanne Scott*

It's hard and confusing enough having children in your home country, but when you're abroad it can be almost impossible to know where to start. Carole helped me navigate my children's needs and was filled with useful insights and resources for me.

When I came to move back home after fifteen years abroad it was a real culture shock and unless you've been in that position nobody else can really see where you're coming from. The world (your home town or country) changes a lot in fifteen years – imperceptible to those who've stayed – so I've loved reading the stories of others who've returned home. *Alex Scheach*

ExpatChild.com has helped me far much more than I expected. Without ExpatChild.com I'd be nowhere, but I'm now much happier and have a great future planned out ahead. *Harry Wallace*

Who better to give advice and information than someone who has been through it all? Fantastic! Emma A

I always recommend Carole at Expatability. Having moved internationally seven time I know how amazing, fascinating… and overwhelming, and isolating it can be. I meet a lot of people who are in the process of moving or have recently arrived in their new country and I always turn them on to Carole and ExpatChild.com

Carole has lots of practical info around moves and school selection, but also on some of the subtler 'soft issues': making friends, moving to another country with kids, having babies in a different culture. *Jill H*

As an expat for eight years, I have often used Carole's site both for help and advice and as a forum to chat about all things expat. It is helpful to talk with others who have country specific advice, but there are also lots of topics on which is helpful to get expat views which are similar across countries and continents. I have discussed subjects such as family breakup and repatriation with others on the site and have also shared my own experiences as a teacher at an international school to assist with questions on expat life and education.

Carole also has a wide range of interests and shares sources and articles on a regular basis. These are then helpful signposts to further resources of help to any expat. *Rachel B*

Fabulous website – full of useful hints and tips, all written with humour and understanding by someone who really DOES know how you feel! *Violet F*

More praise at *expatchild.com*

QUESTIONS TO ASK THE SCHOOL

Repeated from earlier in the book so you can find them easily!

Go with a list of your questions and prioritise them in order of importance to you and your child. The following list will give you some ideas to get you started, although it's good to bear in mind that each school is different, and your requirements may be more specific.

Admissions Criteria

- Is there a place available for my child? If not, how long is the waiting list and when would they realistically be able to start?
- Are there any admissions tests?
- Is there a policy to admit siblings?
- What is the nationality and diversity of their students?
- Does the school advocate and work hard towards inclusivity?

Education

- How many children are in each class? And how many per year group?
- What is the teacher to pupil ratio?
- How are students streamed for ability?
- How is diversity of ability dealt with in the class room, at both ends of the spectrum?
- Are measures in place to assist those with special educational needs and those who are gifted and talented?
- What is the staff turnover at the school like?

- How much homework can be expected?
- What subjects, sciences and languages are offered as exams in the later school years?
- What focus is there on life skills?
- How is religious education taught, if at all? Does this align with your beliefs and wishes?
- What incentives, rewards and discipline systems are in place?
- What do they do if you have a student who is smart but is not performing?
- How do they identify students who need extra help?
- What do they do if a student isn't coping with the workload?
- How do you help a student who is struggling?
- Where do the students go after leaving this school? Is further education facilitated by the school?

Pastoral Care

- How often do parents meet with teachers?
- What contact methods are there between school and parents?
- How do they help new children settle in?
- What do I do if I have a concern about my child?
- What are the mobile phone, internet and social networking policies at school?
- Are parents involved immediately in issues such as bullying, behaviour or other problems?
- How does the school handle bullying? If any staff member says there is no bullying, be suspicious. Either they are lying, or they are unaware due to failures in the anti-bullying system.

Extra-curricular Activities

- Which sports are available and where do they take place?

- What extra music tuition is available? Where and when is it held?

- What other activities are available? Lots of extra-curricular activities indicate that teachers are enthusiastic and prepared to put in an effort.

- Are the extra-curricular activities free, or do they have to be paid for?

- Are there regular school trips?

  Facilities
- Are the buildings and facilities in good condition?

- Do students need to leave school grounds for any activities such as sports? If yes, how is this handled?

Extra Expenses

- What resources do the school provide and what resources are parents expected to pay for?

- Who pays for extra help if your child has special educational needs?

ENDNOTES AND RESOURCES

[1] "Third Culture Kids" by Ruth E. Van Reken, The Telegraph, November 13, 2009
http://www.telegraph.co.uk/education/expateducation/6545869/Third-culture-kids.html

[2] I Am a Triangle, founded by Naomi Hattaway:
http://naomihattaway.com/category/triangle/

[3] Third Culture World: http://www.tckworld.com/useem/home.html

[4] Family of Barack Obama, Wikipedia:
https://en.wikipedia.org/wiki/Family_of_Barack_Obama

[5] "Obama's Third Culture Team", by Ruth Van Reken, The Daily Beast Politics, November 27, 2008
http://www.thedailybeast.com/articles/2008/11/26/obamas-third-culture-team.html

[6] Colin Firth, Wikipedia: https://en.wikipedia.org/wiki/Colin_Firth

[7] "TCKs four times more likely to earn a Bachelor's Degrees"; Third Culture World: http://www.tckworld.com/useem/art2.html

[8] Ruth Van Reken; Cross Cultural Kids
http://www.crossculturalkid.org/about/

[9] International Baccalaureate http://www.ibo.org/

[10] Expatability Chat Group on Facebook:
https://www.facebook.com/groups/ExpatabilityClub/

[11] Pearson Edexcel International Qualifications:
http://qualifications.pearson.com/en/qualifications/edexcel-international-gcses-and-edexcel-certificates.html

[12] Cambridge International Examinations: http://www.cie.org.uk/

[13] InterNations connecting global expats https://www.internations.org/

[14] "Unsociable British Expats" ; The Telegraph, October 24, 2014
http://www.telegraph.co.uk/expat/11193034/Unsociable-British-expats-fail-to-make-local-friends.html

[15] International Youth Exchange Program:
http://www.lionsclubs.org/EN/how-we-serve/youth/youth-camp-and-exchange/index.php

[16] Jill Hodges, Founder of Fire Tech Camp
https://www.firetechcamp.com/

[17] Kari Martindale, Blogger and founder of Karilogue
http://karilogue.com/

[18] "Early Childhood Education and Care in Dubai – an Executive
Summary 2009": https://www.khda.gov.ae/en

[19] Khan Academy: https://www.khanacademy.org/

[20] Conquer Maths: http://www.conquermaths.com/

[21] Kings Tutors, Skype and Online Tutoring:
http://www.kingstutors.co.uk/

[22] BBC Education News
http://news.bbc.co.uk/1/hi/education/8576769.stm and
http://www.bbc.co.uk/news/business-24804804

[23] Home schooling International Status:
https://en.wikipedia.org/wiki/Homeschooling_international_status_an
d_statistics

[24] International Connections Academy
http://www.internationalconnectionsacademy.com/

[25] InterHigh http://interhigh.co.uk/

[26] UK Boarding Schools:
http://www.ukboardingschools.com/advice/schools-and-colleges/

[27] "Boarding School, How Does It Work"; by Tommy Cookson, The
Telegraph, October 12, 2012
http://www.telegraph.co.uk/education/9600063/Boarding-school-
how-does-it-work.html

[28] Independent Schools Council – ISC https://www.isc.co.uk/

[29] The Boarding Schools' Association (BSA)
http://www.boarding.org.uk/

[30] Airport Angels https://www.airportangels.net/

[31] School Trunk http://www.schooltrunk.org/

[32] "Broadening Horizons – The value of the overseas experience," The British Council:
https://www.britishcouncil.org/education/ihe/knowledge-centre/student-mobility/report-broadening-horizons-2015

[33] "Internationalisation of higher education: a cognitive response to the challenges of the twenty first century," J. Mestenhauser et al, University of Minnesota;
http://journals.sagepub.com/doi/abs/10.1177/1028315304263795

[34] Top University Rankings: https://www.topuniversities.com/subject-rankings/2018

[35] British Council: https://study-uk.britishcouncil.org

[36] The Complete University Guide, International Studying Overseas:
http://www.thecompleteuniversityguide.co.uk/international/studying-overseas/

[37] Erasmus+ https://www.erasmusplus.org.uk/frequently-asked-questions/

[38] European Agency for Special Needs and Inclusive Education:
https://www.european-agency.org/

[39] "South Africa: Education Barriers for Children of Disabilities":
Human Rights Watch: https://www.hrw.org/news/2015/08/18/south-africa-education-barriers-children-disabilities

[40] "How Middle East can help Syrian Refugees": by the British Council
https://www.britishcouncil.org/voices-magazine/how-middle-eastern-can-help-children-special-needs

[41] Horizon School Dubai: http://www.horizonschooldubai.com/

[42] "PDF of Aided Special Schools 2015/2016":
http://www.edb.gov.hk/attachment/en/edu-system/special/overview/factsheet/special-edu/spsche15-16.pdf

[43] Children with Special Educational Needs and Disabilities
https://www.gov.uk/children-with-special-educational-needs/special-educational-needs-support

[44] European Agency for Special Needs and Inclusive Education:
https://www.european-agency.org/country-
information/netherlands/national-overview/special-needs-education-
within-the-education-system

[45] Inclusion 4 all http://www.inclusion4all.com/

[46] "How children learn a language – what every parent should know" by
William O Grady
http://linguistlist.org/pubs/cupmag/pdf/O%27grady%20article.pdf

[47] Audible.co.uk https://www.audible.co.uk/

[48] Intercambio https://intercambio.org/

[49] Nikki McArthur https://nikkimcarthur.com

[50] Lynn Schreiber, Founder of Salt and Caramel:
http://www.saltandcaramel.com/

[51] Use It Or Lose It? Study Suggests The Brain Can Remember A
'Forgotten' Language
https://www.sciencedaily.com/releases/2009/09/090924112845.htm

[52] "I am a Triangle – and other thoughts on repatriation": by Naomi
Hattaway http://naomihattaway.com/2013/09/i-am-a-triangle-and-
other-thoughts-on-repatriation/

Printed in Great Britain
by Amazon